LANGUAGE ATTITUDES:
Current Trends and Prospects

P 41
.L33

Roger W. Shuy and Ralph W. Fasold,
Editors

Georgetown University Press, Washington, D.C. 20007

CONTENTS

PREFACE

One of the special interest-group sections of the Twenty-third Georgetown Round Table dealt with the topic of language attitudes. To facilitate and focus an interchange of ideas on this topic, scholars from various disciplines were asked to present accounts of their research to the participants in advance of the meeting. Work in subjective reactions to language (language attitudes, beliefs, values, etc.) is very recent in this country. It is being done by specialists in social psychology, speech, linguistics, psychology, and anthropology. This volume brings together the varied approaches of several researchers in these fields. Their papers may serve as models of various ways of exploring this new and exciting area of language research.

R. W. S. and R. W. F.

SOCIOLINGUISTIC CORRELATES OF SPEECH STYLE IN QUEBEC[1]

ALISON d'ANGLEJAN AND G. RICHARD TUCKER

McGill University

In this study we have examined the state of the French language in Quebec from a sociolinguistic perspective. This research which represents a new dimension in Canadian studies will interest scholars, educators, and administrators for both practical and theoretical reasons. The divergence of Quebec French from standard European French together with the recent attempts of the provincial government to influence the evolution of the language have permitted us to examine one small aspect of people's awareness of the role of language in their lives and their reactions to the attempts at language planning of a modern government in a developed country.

French is today the mother tongue of more than five million Canadians, 75% of whom live in the Province of Quebec. Although enclaves of French-speaking Canadians occur throughout the country, English is rapidly replacing French as the language of the French Canadian ethnic group in all areas other than Quebec, a trend also noted in the French-speaking areas in the northern part of the United States.

In Quebec, the high proportion of French Canadians plus the strong retention of French in the province (only 1.6% of Quebec's French ethnic population reported English as their mother tongue in 1961) has served to maintain the position of French as one of Canada's two official languages and to provide an important shield against linguistic and cultural assimilation (Lieberson 1970).

Although the British North America Act of 1867 recognized French and English as the two official languages of Canada, there is abundant

1

evidence (Porter 1958, Royal Commission on Bilingualism and Bi-culturalism 1965) that the French language occupied a minor position in Canada and that even in Quebec, French Canadians were under-represented in the higher echelons of business and industry where English became firmly entrenched as the working language. The eruption of terrorist activities in the early 1960's brought to light both the feelings of resentment held by many French Canadians with respect to their inferior status and the separatist aspirations of cer-tain segments of their society. The following ten years which have been marked by sporadic outbursts of terrorism and the birth of an official Quebec separatist party have seen a parallel acceleration in language policy developments at both the federal and provincial levels.

In their historical survey of the development of language policy in Quebec, Pinault and Ladouceur (1971) pointed out that more has been done in the past ten years to guarantee the maintenance and develop-ment of French as the de jure and de facto working language of the province than during the preceding 190 years. For example, it is now mandatory for all English-speaking children to acquire a working knowledge of French within their school curriculum; a working knowl-edge of French has replaced Canadian citizenship as a requirement for certain professional licenses; and direct pressure has been ex-erted on large businesses and industries to collaborate with the government to make French the working language of employees at all levels.

In view of the significant role which French has played in preserv-ing the people of Quebec and their culture from assimilation, and the relationship between language and nationalistic movements throughout the world, it is not surprising to find that language matters occupy a position of priority on the Quebec political and educational scene.

The French spoken in Quebec today by all but a small academic and professional elite differs at all levels of linguistic analysis from the accepted prestige form of the language spoken in France. Spilka (1970) attributed the high status of this standard model which has evolved from the Ile-de-France dialect to three main factors: (1) early and successful efforts at language standardization on the part of the State (the Académie Française entrusted with the defense and preservation of the French language was founded in 1635, and pub-lished its first dictionary in 1644; (2) the considerable prestige en-joyed by France and by French culture throughout the world; and (3) the absence of any serious political and economic challenge to France's superior position by other French-speaking nations. French colonies and former colonies have always remained subordinate to the mother country; in Canada, particularly, the French-speaking community has been ascribed an inferior status.

Denis (1949) described the evolution of the French language in Canada following the British conquest and the departure of the French-speaking elite. Cut off from contact with other French language centers, Canadian French quickly became archaic and offered little resistance to the influence of English. By the end of the 19th century, the contamination of French by borrowings from English reached such proportions that public campaigns were organized to awaken French Canadians to the fact that their language was in danger. These campaigns and corrective movements were ineffective in the face of the growing influence of the English language press and eventually of radio and television. These events led Valin (1970) to remark that if Quebec French was left to evolve naturally it could become unintelligible to speakers of standard French.

In 1961 the Quebec government established an Office de la langue française (OLF). This agency was assigned the task of revitalizing French in Quebec by bringing it closer to standard French and by upgrading the language of the underprivileged classes. The OLF regularly disseminates normative bulletins to educational institutions, businesses, and mass media which draw attention to the specific differences distinguishing Quebec French from standard French and provide appropriate standard French vocabulary lists to replace certain canadianisms and anglicisms now in common use.

In its first official publication, Cahier No. 1, the OLF stated that if the French language in Quebec is to survive the pressures of an English-speaking North American milieu, it must adhere to the same norms which prevail in other large francophone countries. No variation in morphology or syntax can be tolerated; phonetic and lexical variation should be reduced to an absolute minimum. It is interesting to note that this document does not deal with language variation in the objective terms of modern linguistics but is highly subjective and punctuated with value judgments of the following nature:

> Nous devons nous efforcer de produire les trentesix phonèmes (du français) avec la plus grande pureté possible. Mais nos prononciations vicieuses, notre relâchement articulatoire . . . nous écartent trop de la bonne voie à suivre dans ce domaine. Trop nombreux sont les sons que nous réalisons de façon défectueuse . . . Ce sont autant d'exemples de prononciation qui exigent un travail de redressement articulatoire . . . Quand à notre relâchement articulatoire dans le discours, il est absolument inacceptable (Cahier No. 1, p. 8, 1965).

Attitudes such as these are not new, and the tone is strongly reminiscent of that which has characterized pronouncements of the

Académie Française and an extensive list of French grammarians
dating back to the sixteenth century.

According to Harmer (1954), the French at all levels of society
display an intense interest in their own language and show remarkably
little tolerance or sympathy toward either regional or social class
deviation from the prestige form. It is understandable, therefore,
that French Canadians who are now attempting to establish and
strengthen cultural ties with France as a bulwark against the pressures of North America may feel sensitive and somewhat insecure
with respect to their 'nonstandard' dialect. Miner (1939) remarked
that the rural French Canadian is usually apologetic about his speech.
Corrective measures have succeeded in making him lose pride in his
language and he has no real basis for judging which of the words he
uses are standard French and which are not.

The results of a number of empirical studies conducted in several
countries support these generalizations. They suggest that regional
dialect variables may come to elicit socially conditioned value judgments which in turn affect the attitudes of listeners toward speakers
from various backgrounds. A speaker may be judged favorably or
unfavorably by the prestige of the dialect that he speaks. Markel,
Eisler, and Reese (1967) demonstrated that in the United States
regional dialect is a significant factor in judging personality from
speech style. Giles (1970) reported similar findings in England,
while Tucker (1968) reported that speakers of American English were
viewed more favorably than speakers of Filipino English or of Tagalog
by listeners in the Philippines. The findings most relevant to this
study were those reported by Lambert (1967). French and English
Canadian university students were asked to rate the personality charac
teristics of ten speakers--five English and five French. In reality,
five bilingual speakers were used with each speaker appearing in two
guises. English students evaluated the English-speaking guises more
favorably on most traits, while French students not only evaluated
English guises more favorably than French guises, but also evaluated
the French guises significantly less favorably than the English students did.

Labov's (1966) extensive study of the social stratification of speech
in New York City drew attention to the importance of the relationship
between speech and social class. Speakers from different social
levels are characterized by distinctive phonological, syntactic, and
lexical features which are easily identified by linguistically naive
judges and which may be used by these judges as a basis for evaluating the speakers. Ellis (1967) showed that naive judges speaking
one regional dialect of American English can accurately identify the
social status of persons speaking different dialects.

An additional aspect of the relationship between language and social class was brought to light in Labov's (1967) study of social mobility which indicated that upwardly mobile people tend to adopt the linguistic style of the socioeconomic group just above their own. Brown (1969) reported similar findings in a French Canadian study. The speech styles of different socioeconomic levels can be accurately discerned by listeners, mainly on the basis of a gross upper class-lower class dichotomy. French Canadians tend to model their speech on those with whom they identify, i.e. those who are upwardly mobile adopt upper-class speech features.

Some of the possible psychological implications of speech style were discussed by Halliday (1968) who pointed out that the socioregional pattern of dialect distribution gives rise to socially conditioned moral and aesthetic value judgments. He warned that when attitudes of inferiority come to be shared by those who themselves speak the nonstandard or stigmatized dialect, and no other, they become harmful.

A speaker who is made ashamed of his own language habits suffers a basic injury as a human being; to make anyone, especially a child feel so ashamed is as indefensible as to make him feel ashamed of the colour of his skin (Halliday 1968:165).

One might speculate that particular attention should be paid to these possible psychological implications in Quebec where French Canadians have been exposed to continual negative value judgments about the quality of their speech. To date, however, researchers have concentrated on the identification and description of the speech style of French Canadians from different geographic and social strata (e.g. Charbonneau 1955, Ellis 1965, Gendron 1966) while very few studies have examined sociolinguistic correlates of the linguistic variables. The one preliminary investigation in this area conducted by Chiasson-Lavoie and Laberge (1971) did find evidence of linguistic insecurity among lower-class French Canadians in Montreal.

The scarcity of data concerning possible correlates of speech style in French Canada together with the salience of language as a political and educational issue in the province motivated the present investigation. As a result of a pilot study which we conducted in Montreal in 1970 with 75 French Canadian junior-college students and teachers, the following areas were chosen for investigation:

(1) The awareness in people of regional and social dialect variation.
(2) The importance of language in general as a factor in social and academic success.
(3) The attitudes of people toward their own speech style and that of speakers from other social classes and regions.

(4) The willingness of people to accept standard European French as the prestige model.
(5) The reactions of people toward the systematic attempts by the government to standardize their language.

The present study was designed to investigate these questions, in a preliminary way, with groups of subjects from different occupations and different geographic locations throughout the province of Quebec.

Method

Subjects. All subjects (Ss) for this investigation were French Canadians who had been born and brought up in Quebec. Since many of the OLF materials are directed to schools, and since the educational system is traditionally one of the main vehicles by which language policy decisions are implemented, groups of teachers and students at the high-school level were selected as subjects. Students were from working class and lower-middle class backgrounds. In addition, groups of factory workers were included to study the reactions of Ss who might be less language conscious than the others. To obtain a relatively representative distribution of Ss and to be able to look at the possible effects of regional variation on language attitudes, Ss were selected from three geographical locations in Quebec: (1) Montreal, a large cosmopolitan, multilingual city; (2) Alma, a rural, predominantly French-speaking community; and (3) Quebec, a small monolingual city, and the Provincial capital. The sample is described in Table 1.

TABLE 1. Distribution of sample.

Location	Occupation	Male	Female	Total	Avg. age	Avg. no. yrs. experience
Montreal	Students	11	16	27	16.33	..
	Teachers	17	10	27	..	6.48
	Workers	13	14	27	24.58	..
Alma	Students	10	17	27	17.35	..
	Teachers	16	11	27	..	7.30
	Workers	12	15	27	30.81	..
Quebec	Students	11	16	27	16.93	..
	Teachers	20	7	27	..	7.15
	Workers	10	17	27	23.63	..
	Total	120	123	243		

Materials. Two complementary measures were used to assess the language attitudes of the Ss. In view of the low degree of constancy between attitude measures and actual behavior reported in studies reviewed by Agheyisi and Fishman (1970), we hoped that comparisons of the data resulting from two contrasting measures might help to validate the findings.

The first measure was a questionnaire comprising forty multiple choice and semantic differential type items. The appropriateness of each question as well as the format was determined in a pilot study. The questions focused on Ss' awareness of speech style differences, the importance they attributed to language, their awareness of government language policy, etc.

As a complementary measure, Ss were asked to evaluate the speech styles of twelve speakers and to indicate their probable occupational status. Samples were recorded from four lower-class and four upper-class French Canadians and from four Europeans. All were male, native speakers of French selected on the basis of their occupational status and country of origin. The lower-class speakers were a janitor, a maintenance man, a parking attendant, and a carpenter. They ranged in age from 40 to 50 years. All were native Montrealers. Upper-class speakers were a psychiatrist, an architect, and two university professors, all from Montreal, ranging in age from 30 to 45 years. European speakers were three French university students and a business man, ranging in age from 23 to 35. The voices were arranged in random order for the stimulus tape.

We decided for this portion of the study to obtain a sample of free speech rather than a sample of reading which allows variation in phonology but controls the use of syntax and lexical items. Giles (1970) draws an important distinction between the perception of accent as opposed to dialect. Dialect implies variation from the standard code at most levels of linguistic analysis, whereas 'accent' merely implies a manner of pronunciation with grammatical, syntactical, morphological, and lexical levels being regarded as more or less commensurate with the standard. Since this study is concerned with dialect variation and not reactions to accent only, a sample of free speech seemed the most appropriate stimulus. Furthermore, Agheyisi and Fishman (1970) suggest that in the typical 'matched-guise' experiment when judges evaluate speakers on the basis of a sample of reading, they may well be reacting to things such as the congruity, or lack of it, between the speaker, the topic, and the particular language variety. They feel that this congruity, or incongruity, should be studied rather than obscured.

The speakers used in this study were interviewed separately and informally on a specific topic, a record-breaking blizzard which occurred in Montreal during the first week of March 1971. This

topic permitted them considerable freedom of expression. A 30 to
40 second sample of uninterrupted speech was selected from the output of each speaker. The final tape consisted of thirteen voices:
four exemplars from each of the three categories and one additional
French Canadian voice at the beginning of the tape which served as a
'practice' voice to acquaint Ss with the type of judgments they were to
make for the following twelve voices.

The Ss were asked to make a series of rapid, subjective value
judgments about each speaker: How intelligent does he sound? How
likeable; educated; ambitious; tough; etc. ? Is his speech style an
asset to him or a liability? What type of job would he probably hold?
The Ss were encouraged to make their ratings using seven-point
semantic differential-type scales quickly and intuitively.

An additional content-free tape recording was prepared in which
the same speakers counted from one to twenty. Ellis (1967) found
that a 20 second sample of counting was a sufficiently powerful stimulus to enable Ss to make accurate social class predictions. For this
phase of the task, Ss were asked to indicate the probability that each
speaker belonged to an upper or a lower occupational status group.

Testing procedure. Students in the three settings were group-
tested in their respective classrooms. Teachers and workers were
tested either individually or in small groups. The testing was carried
out by two male French Canadian university students. All Ss first
completed the objective questionnaire, then listened and evaluated
one by one the thirteen voices on the free speech tape followed by the
thirteen samples of content-controlled speech.

Method of data analysis. A variety of formal and informal data
analyses were used in the present study. For the questionnaire, the
frequencies of response by each of the nine groups of Ss were tabulated and converted to percentages for the multiple choice questions.
The data for the questions answered with semantic differential rating
scales were analyzed using separate two-way analyses of variance.
The independent variables were geographic location (Montreal, Alma,
and Quebec) and occupation (student, teacher, and worker).

For the voice data, separate three-way analyses of variance, with
repeated measures, were used for each rating scale. Ratings for
the four exemplars of each voice category were first averaged to obtain a single score for each speech style. The independent variables
were geographic location (Montreal, Alma, and Quebec), occupation
(student, teacher, and worker), and speech style (standard European
French, upper-class French Canadian, and lower-class French
Canadian).

Results and discussion

The data from the objective questionnaire and from the voice evaluations will be presented separately. Items from different parts of the questionnaire have been grouped according to topical area to facilitate discussion, and we have tried to draw attention to certain of the more general and consistent themes which occur throughout the data. We did not pay particular attention to significant main effects for location or to interactions involving location since the biographical information from our Ss revealed that many of them did not originally come from the locations in which they were interviewed.

Awareness of social class stratification. The responses to the first four questions indicated that a majority of the Ss from the three occupations in each geographical setting are conscious of speech variation. Underlying this consensus were minor variations in the patterns of responses. For example, the teachers in each setting showed relatively more awareness of variation (95% answered positively) than did the students (85%) or the workers (75%) when asked if they noticed that certain people in their community speak a style of French different from their own.

Furthermore, when Ss were asked to classify various occupational groups according to speech style, very clear patterns emerged. All Ss tended to cluster lawyers with university professors and radio announcers; and bus drivers with mailmen and janitors in a separate group. However, some of them assigned the occupation of bank clerk to one category; and some, to the other. This is not surprising since this latter occupation represents a point midway between high occupational status and low status according to Blishen (1958).

The Ss tended to classify their own speech style differentially according to their occupation. The following summary indicates the most frequently occurring groupings of Ss' own speech style by occupation and region:

Montreal	Students: bus driver or bank clerk
	Teachers: lawyer
	Workers: bus driver
Alma	Students: bank clerk
	Teachers: bank clerk
	Workers: bus driver
Quebec	Students: bank clerk
	Teachers: lawyer
	Workers: bank clerk

Apart from Montreal and Quebec teachers who viewed their own speech style as similar to that of lawyers, the highest category on the Blishen scale, most respondents grouped their speech with that of lower occupational status groups. This probably represents an accurate judgment since the students and workers came from lower-middle class and working class families. These data provide evidence that Ss do perceive clearly distinguishable differences in the speech of lower- and upper-class groups. The implications of these differences will be discussed after the voice data have been presented.

When asked to give the names of public figures whose speech style they particularly like or dislike, Ss in all groups mentioned prominent political figures (e.g. Robert Bourassa, Réal Caouette, René Lévèsque Pierre Trudeau) who have appeared frequently on television at election time and whose speech style is familiar to most French Canadians. All groups showed a preference for the educated French Canadian speech model. Two political figures, Réal Caouette and Camil Samson, speakers of the low prestige nonstandard 'joual' form of Quebec French appeared consistently in the 'dislike' category. Pierre Trudeau who speaks a European style standard French was mentioned frequently in both the 'like' and 'dislike' categories. While these responses show interesting patterns and appear to complement the data from the two previous questions, it should be remembered that they may well be the reflection of individual political biases.

Awareness of regional variation. The responses to another series of questions indicated that a majority of Ss have encountered speakers from other dialect regions in Quebec, and are conscious of this type of variation in speech style. Table 2 provides a breakdown of the responses to three of these questions in percentages. Members of all groups report having experienced difficulty in understanding speakers from other regions (question B) with the highest figure reported by the Montreal sample (64%). This is understandable since Montrealers would more likely be travelling to areas of the province where speech deviates from the metropolitan norm than the Ss from Quebec and Alma who would perhaps be visiting Montreal, and who may have had prior exposure to the Montreal variety of French on radio or TV.

Responses indicated that Ss have little difficulty in making themselves understood when visiting other parts of the province (question C). Relative to other groups, workers from Alma reported slightly more difficulty in making themselves understood which suggests that the Lac St. Jean dialect differs noticeably from that of Montreal or Quebec.

Furthermore, all teachers and most students in the three areas indicated that they have encountered French-speaking Europeans

TABLE 2. Percentage of affirmative responses.

Questions:		A	B	C
Montreal	Students	93	64	26
	Teachers	89	80	28
	Workers	78	48	13
	$\overline{X}=$	87	64	22
Alma	Students	81	42	8
	Teachers	100	52	11
	Workers	89	31	30
	$\overline{X}=$	90	42	16
Quebec	Students	85	40	17
	Teachers	100	40	8
	Workers	81	38	22
	$\overline{X}=$	89	39	16

A = Avez-vous eu l'occasion de visiter d'autres régions du Québec?
B = Si oui, avez-vous eu du mal à comprendre le français qu'on
  parle dans certaines de ces régions?
C = Avez-vous eu du mal à vous faire comprendre dans certaines de
  ces régions?

(see Table 3). A surprising finding is that nearly 50% of Montreal
workers claimed that they had not met any Europeans (question D).
This seems unlikely since the probability of encountering Europeans
is greater in Montreal than in either Alma or Quebec. These Ss have
probably met Europeans but may have remained unaware of this fact.
All groups have experienced difficulty in understanding Europeans
(question E), with the highest figure (44%) reported by students in
Alma. Furthermore, all groups reported some degree of difficulty
in making themselves understood by Europeans (question F), with
Alma students again reporting the highest percentage (57%).

Attitudes toward speech style. Eight questions probed Ss' opinions
about the existence of a recognized prestige form of French in Quebec,
what this form might be and whether they are satisfied with their own
speech style.
  All groups report being moderately, but not entirely, satisfied
with their own speech style ($\overline{X}=3.76$ on a 7-point scale). There were
no significant occupation or location differences among the groups.
The fact that Ss were not more satisfied with their speech style may

TABLE 3. Percentage of affirmative responses.

Questions:		D	E	F
Montreal	Students	89	28	42
	Teachers	100	23	19
	Workers	52	40	29
	X =	80	30	30
Alma	Students	93	44	57
	Teachers	100	37	30
	Workers	85	28	28
	X =	93	36	38
Quebec	Students	89	19	27
	Teachers	100	17	20
	Workers	59	30	38
	X =	83	22	28

D = Avez-vous eu l'occasion de rencontrer des européens de langue française (français, belges, suisses, etc.)?
E = Si oui, avez-vous eu du mal à comprendre le français parlé par ces personnes?
F = Avez-vous eu du mal à vous faire comprendre par ces personnes?

reflect accurately the feelings of people from these social strata. It may, on the other hand, be a consequence of the various speech improvement movements which have tended to make French Canadians self-conscious about their speech style.

The responses of all groups indicate that Ss listen to Radio-Canada with Ss from Alma listening relatively more frequently than groups in the other areas (Alma $\overline{X}$ = 1.78, Quebec $\overline{X}$ = 2.26, Montreal $\overline{X}$ = 2.46; F = 4.80, df = 2/234, p < .01). This probably reflects the fact that there are no private radio or TV stations broadcasting in Alma, whereas many do exist in Montreal and Quebec.

The French spoken on Radio-Canada, a variety close to standard European French, represents the best form of Quebec French ($\overline{X}$ = 2.53) for Ss from all areas. Among those who reported that they do not agree that Radio-Canada represents the prestige model, there is no consensus concerning an alternative although Ss in Montreal frequently proposed private radio and TV stations whose announcers incidentally tend to speak Quebec style French.

The responses of Ss show that they feel their speech has been only moderately influenced by Radio-Canada (Students $\overline{X}$ = 4.78, Workers

$\overline{X}$ = 4.44, Teachers $\overline{X}$ = 3.65; F = 6.69, df = 2/234, p < .01). No particular significance is attached to this difference which may reflect a reluctance on the part of students to admit to being influenced by 'the establishment'.

When asked to indicate how their own speech style differs from the best form of French in Quebec, all groups rated vocabulary and pronunciation as the most important sources of difference. Grammar was rated least different by all groups. This finding is consistent with data reported by Chiasson-Lavoie and Laberge (1971) that Ss in Montreal were less conscious of grammatical variables than phonological ones. However, it is also likely that teachers, at least, might feel that their grammar coincides with the standard form, while workers might be unaware of their deviation in this area. A summary of the responses to this question appears in Table 4.

TABLE 4. Responses expressed in percentages.

Q: De quelle façon votre langage diffère-t-il de la meilleure forme de français au Québec?						
R:		N	P	G	V	I
Montreal						
Students		15	30	22	74	15
Teachers		19	52	4	37	44
Workers		0	58	0	35	31
	$\overline{X}$ =	11	47	9	49	30
Alma						
Students		0	48	19	81	41
Teachers		15	44	7	52	33
Workers		15	26	11	52	33
	$\overline{X}$ =	10	39	12	62	36
Quebec						
Students		7	48	11	52	22
Teachers		15	37	11	59	41
Workers		15	33	11	52	26
	$\overline{X}$ =	12	39	11	54	30

N = None; P = Pronunciation; G = Grammar; V = Vocabulary;
I = Intonation

The Ss refused to accept the cliches that the French of Quebec is not so nice as European French ($\overline{X}$ = 4.77) and that Parisian French is the best French ($\overline{X}$ = 5.21). However, they did not respond at the extreme negative end of the scale which suggests that their disagreement with the statements is not absolute. This was one of the few places on either the objective or subjective questionnaires where Quebec French was not viewed less favorably than standard French and suggests that contrasting types of measures may probe different levels of the Ss' awareness.

There was a significant interaction in response to the statement that Quebec French is not so nice as European French between occupational group and location ($F = 3.83$, df $= 4/234$, $p < .01$) with students in Montreal showing the greatest disagreement with the cliche and students in Quebec the least.

The statement that people make fun of someone who speaks too well was questioned by all groups ($\overline{X} = 3.85$). There was, however, a significant difference among the means for the three locations (Montreal $\overline{X} = 4.14$, Alma $\overline{X} = 4.16$, Quebec $\overline{X} = 3.26$; $F = 4.76$, df $= 2/234$, $p < .01$) with Quebec Ss indicating a neutral position in contrast to the greater disagreement expressed by both the Montreal and Alma groups.

The Ss expressed only slight agreement with the statement that one is judged more by his way of speaking than by his intelligence although there was a significant difference among the responses by the three occupational groups (Students $\overline{X} = 3.17$, Teachers $\overline{X} = 3.43$, Workers $\overline{X} = 2.37$; $F = 7.90$, df $= 2/234$, $p < .01$). Note that the workers judged speech to be relatively more important than intelligence; a trend which was reversed on some other questions.

Finally, Ss reported that they consider speech style to be only moderately related to academic success. The difference among the mean scores for the occupational groups was significant (Students $\overline{X} = 2.80$, Teachers $\overline{X} = 3.64$, Workers $\overline{X} = 3.27$; $F = 3.59$, df $= 2/234$, $p < .05$) with students tending to express the greatest agreement that an educated person speaks better than an uneducated one.

Importance attributed to speech style. Ss clearly rated language as secondary in importance to both personality and intelligence as a factor which affects scholastic or university success, success in obtaining a good job, and success in making friends on a series of four questions. A summary of the rankings by group is presented in Table 5. This general pattern of findings, despite their previously expressed awareness of the direct relationship between speech style and occupational status, was not at all surprising since language must certainly be a less 'visible' factor than either intelligence or personality; and in fact we would not expect our linguistically naive Ss to show a conscious awareness of the subtle nature of the relationship between language and intelligence or language and social class.

TABLE 5. Summary classification of dress (D), intelligence (I),
language (L), personality (P), and social class (S) by
rank order of importance.

	Rank	Montreal S T W			Alma S T W			Quebec S T W		
Success at school	1	I	I	I	I	I	I	I	I	I
	2	P	P	L	P	P	P	P	P	P
	3	L	L	P	L	L	L	L	L	L
	4	S	S	S	S	S	S	S	S	S
	5	D	D	D	D	D	D	D	D	D
Success at university	1	I	I	I	I	I	I	I	I	I
	2	P	P	L	P	P	P	P	P	P
	3	L	L	P	L	L	L	L	L	L
	4	S	S	S	S	S	S	S	S	S
	5	D	D	D	D	D	D	D	D	D
Success in finding a good job	1	P	P	P	P	P	P	P	P	P
	2	I	L	L	I	L	I	I	L	I
	3	L	I	I	L	I	L	L	I	L
	4	D	D	D	D	D	D	D	S	D
	5	S	S	S	S	S	S	S	D	S
Success in making friends	1	P	P	P	P	P	P	P	P	P
	2	L	I	I	I	I	L	I	I	I
	3	I	L	L	L	L	I	L	L	L
	4	S	D	D	S	S	S	S	S	S
	5	D	S	S	D	D	D	D	D	D

S = Students; T = Teachers; W = Workers

The evolution of language and language policy. Objective inferences
about language change may be made by comparing the phonology, syntax or lexicon, for example, of the French spoken today in Montreal
with that spoken two hundred years ago. A series of very systematic
statements could be made to describe the nature of that change or
even the change during the past fifty years. From a sociolinguistic
perspective, however, it may be more interesting to examine people's
awareness of language as a static or dynamic entity and their reactions to attempts to influence language change.

In response to the question whether language stays the same or
changes, 80% of the respondents agreed that it changes. However, a
disproportionately high number of workers in Montreal (33%) reported

that it remains the same. This finding supports our earlier speculation that workers as a group may be less language conscious than
our other Ss.

Respondents from all groups provided diverse and often extremely
perceptive suggestions about the forces that might cause language to
change. Almost all Ss cited the effect of radio and TV which suggests
that their responses to the earlier question concerning Radio-Canada's
influence on their speech may have been an understatement. Some of
the other factors listed by Ss were improved educational opportunities, the effects of immigration, an awareness of poor speech habits,
changes in generation and cultural isolation.

When the focus was shifted from language in general to Quebec
French in particular, approximately 80% of the Ss again indicated an
awareness that the French language in Quebec is evolving. Once more,
workers differed from students and teachers with 29% of Montreal
workers and 28% of the Quebec workers reporting that they do not
think that the French language is evolving.

Having established that most Ss view language as dynamic, we next
probed to determine whether they believed that it was possible and
desirable to influence this natural process. Although the Ss in general believed that it is possible to influence the natural development
of language ($\overline{X}$ = 2.37), there was a significant interaction between
occupation and location (F = 3.18, df = 4/234, p < .05). The Quebec
teachers were relatively less sure ($\overline{X}$ = 3.22) than the others that
language evolution could be externally influenced, while the Quebec
workers were relatively more sure ($\overline{X}$ = 1.85).

The Ss expressed a slightly more conservative view when asked
whether they felt that it was desirable to influence the natural evolution of language ($\overline{X}$ = 2.90). There was, however, a significant main
effect for location (F = 5.11, df = 2/234; p < .01) with Montreal students being relatively more conservative ($\overline{X}$ = 3.41) than those from
Quebec ($\overline{X}$ = 2.72) or Alma ($\overline{X}$ = 2.58). Once again there was a significant interaction between occupation and location (F = 3.72, df =
4/234, p < .01). The Montreal students in particular felt that it is
inappropriate to interfere with the natural development of language.
This is consistent with their responses to the earlier question where
they reported that their speech was relatively uninfluenced by Radio-
Canada. Again, these data may reflect anti-establishment feelings.

Finally, there was consensus ($\overline{X}$ = 1.85) that the French spoken in
Quebec does need improvement, although there was a significant
location effect (F = 3.17, df = 2/234, p < .05) and a significant interaction between location and occupation (F = 4.08, df = 4/234, p < .01).
As Figure 1 indicates, the Montreal students are relatively less
adamant in their belief that the language needs improvement ($\overline{X}$ = 2.81)
than Ss from the other eight groups.

FIGURE 1.   Interaction between occupation and location in response
to whether Quebec French needs improvement.

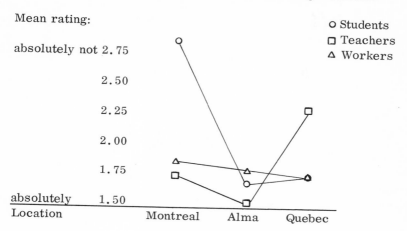

As a follow-up to the previous question, all Ss chose vocabulary
and pronunciation most frequently (see Table 6) when asked to indicate
what they considered to be the weaknesses, if any, of Quebec French.
Grammar was in third place, followed by intonation.   The workers in
all locations chose pronunciation more frequently than vocabulary.
These findings again coincide with those of Chiasson-Lavoie and
Laberge (1971), and indicate that people are less conscious of deviant
grammatical features in their speech.   They are probably quite unaware of the intrusion of certain English syntactic structures in their
French (e.g. Je n'ai jamais vu des choses qui vaillent la peine de se
battre pour).   Their reported high level of awareness of phonology as
a weakness was complemented by the voice data where Ss made accurate social class distinctions after listening to a sample of speakers
counting aloud.

TABLE 6.   Perceived weaknesses in Quebec French by rank order
of importance.

	Montreal S T W	Alma S T W	Quebec S T W
Pronunciation	2 2 1	1 1 1	2 1 1
Vocabulary	1 1 2	2 2 2	1 2 2
Grammar	3 3 3	3 3 3	3 3 3
Intonation	4 4 4	4 4 4	4 4 4
S = Students; T = Teachers; W = Workers			

The responses of the Ss to this series of questions revealed that they are aware of language variation, that they believe that languages are dynamic entities which evolve naturally; but that it may be possible to overtly influence the natural course of the evolution of a language. Furthermore, the Ss felt that the French spoken in Quebec was in need of improvement. In view of the fact that the government established the OLF in 1961 to promote and maintain the French language in Quebec, we next decided to probe Ss' awareness of this organization and their views about who, in general, should assume responsibility for language planning in Quebec.

A very clear pattern emerged when Ss indicated that European linguists and universities were not appropriate organizations for effecting language policy.

This reaction interested us since we had included the category 'European linguist' in the questionnaire when our attention was drawn to headlines in the Montreal press stating that the government had hired a team of European linguists to teach French Canadians correct 'anguage usage.

Students and teachers most frequently cited parents, teachers, and then the government in that order as the group to effect language policy while the workers most frequently selected teachers followed by the government. This latter finding suggests that the workers may feel themselves relatively incapable of helping their own children and implies an awareness on their part that their own parents were unable to help them. The rankings by each group are reported in Table 7.

TABLE 7. 'Qui devrait s'occuper d'améliorer our de préserver la langue française au Québec?'

The choices of each group expressed in rank order:			
	Students	Teachers	Workers
Government	3	3	2
Teachers	2	2	1
Parents	1	1	3
European linguists	5	5	5
University	4	4	4

Four questions probe directly the Ss' awareness of the activities of the OLF. Our pilot study conducted in Montreal revealed that students and teachers at the junior college level were generally aware of the OLF's existence, although they were occasionally unsure about the nature of its mandate which some thought to be the promotion of unilingualism. The data from the present study show that only 56% of the teachers, 32% of the students, and 26% of the workers had heard of the OLF. The low percentage for the workers suggests to us that the question may have been incorrectly phrased for this group. We should probably have questioned their exposure to the OLF's publicity to make French the working language of industry. Indeed, factory workers whom we tested referred to this campaign and occasionally thought our investigation was a part of it.

In general, those Ss who indicated awareness of the OLF also understood and supported its objectives and found them realistic. There was less tendency than in our pilot study to cite the promotion of unilingualism as an OLF goal.

Finally three questions were designed to probe Ss' feelings of insecurity or defensiveness with respect to their language. A majority of Ss (87%) reported that they generally accept correction and try to adjust their speech habits when errors are pointed out to them by a Quebecer; however, only 50% will accept corrections from a European. Since many workers previously reported that they had not met Europeans, this potentially interesting difference must be interpreted with caution.

The Ss' responses indicate a desire for 'correct' speech, (e.g Qu'est ce qui a le plus d'importance pour vous: que votre prononciation soit 'correcte' ou que votre prononciation garde son caractere Quebecois). Correctness over ethnicity in grammar was favored by 75% of all Ss, while a slightly lower percentage (70%) preferred correctness over ethnicity in vocabulary. In contrast, only 60% of the Ss indicated a preference for 'correct' pronunciation over 'Quebec' pronunciation. These data again lend credence to the belief that French Canadians are clearly aware of the phonological differences between their language and standard French, but relatively unaware of the extent to which their syntax diverges from standard patterns. In this respect, the normative bulletins of the OLF may be serving a particularly valuable function.

In the preceding section, Ss were asked to consider specific topics and express objective opinions. The data which we are about to present represent an attempt to probe, in a more subtle manner, their subjective reactions to variations in speech style and to substantiate, if possible, some of the previous findings.

Voice data. The Ss listened to speech samples collected from upper- (UFC) and lower-class (LFC) French Canadian speakers and from standard European French (SEF) speakers. They listened first to samples of spontaneous conversation, then to the same speakers counting aloud from one to twenty. After listening to each sample, Ss were asked to evaluate the speaker using selected semantic differential adjective scales and to answer a series of questions about the person's speech style.

On the basis of previous research (e. g. Labov 1966, Lambert 1967), we predicted that significant interactions would occur between the occupational group of our Ss and the speech styles of the stimulus voices which they judged. Furthermore, we predicted that there would be significant main effects for speech style.

The first noteworthy finding is the fact that Ss differentially assigned occupations to the speakers on the basis of their speech style ($F = 245.99$, df = 2/234, p < .01). All Ss tended to rate SEF speakers higher on the occupational scale ($\overline{X} = 2.18$) than they rated the UFC ($\overline{X} = 3.30$) or the LFC speakers ($\overline{X} = 3.50$). They appeared to differentiate more clearly between European and Canadian speakers, in general, than they did between the UFC and LFC speakers. This pattern recurs with other measures. In addition, there was a significant group effect ($F = 4.17$, df = 2/234, p < .05) with the workers, in general, tending to rate all speakers lower on the occupational scale ($\overline{X} = 3.09$) than did the students ($\overline{X} = 2.96$) or the teachers ($\overline{X} = 2.94$).

A methodological problem may account for the fact that the distinctions between the UFC and the LFC speakers were not more pronounced. The differences might have been greater had the Ss been asked to make a dichotomous choice between clearly upper-class and clearly lower-class occupations (cf. Brown 1969). Furthermore, our attempt for purposes of this analysis to adapt Blishen's (1958) social class categories to a 7-point scale, including intermediary and perhaps ambiguous categories such as bank clerk and radio announcer, may have precluded our obtaining more clearly defined differences.

When making judgments after listening to the counting samples, the Ss again reacted differentially and appropriately. A significant main effect for speech style ($F = 579.03$, df = 2/234, p < .01) was obtained when the Ss were asked whether the speaker was likely to be a mailman, bus driver, or janitor. The SEF speakers were perceived as least likely to hold this type of occupation ($\overline{X} = 5.57$), with the UFC next ($\overline{X} = 3.36$), and the LFC perceived as most likely ($\overline{X} = 2.39$). Furthermore, there was a significant interaction between occupation and speech style ($F = 15.06$, df = 4/234, p < .01) which is shown in Figure 2.

A complementary set of findings emerged when the Ss were asked whether these same speakers were likely to be lawyers, professors, or dentists. Again, there was a significant main effect for speech style ($F = 632.47$, df = 2/234, p < .01) with the SEF speakers being perceived as most likely to have these occupations ($\overline{X} = 2.46$), followed by the UFC ($\overline{X} = 4.60$), and the LFC ($\overline{X} = 5.71$) speakers. There was also a significant interaction between occupation and speech style ($F = 10.08$, df = 4/234, p < .01) which is shown in

FIGURE 2. Significant interaction between occupation and speech
style in Ss' ability to discriminate lower-class
speakers.

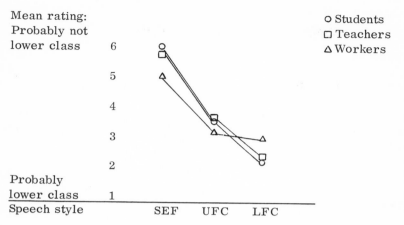

FIGURE 3. Significant interaction between occupation and speech
style in Ss' ability to discriminate upper-class
speakers.

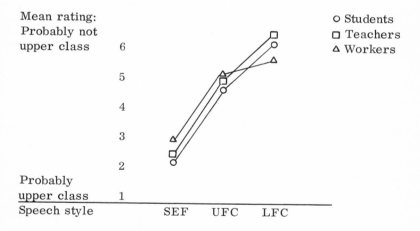

Figure 3. The patterns for these two significant interactions are remarkably similar. All Ss clearly discriminated between speakers on
the basis of speech style although the workers appear to distinguish
European from Canadian speakers while the students and teachers
make finer discriminations among all three categories of speakers.

The Ss' reactions to the spontaneous speech samples revealed the existence of a powerful main effect attributable to speech style for all five adjective rating scales. The SEF speakers were consistently rated more intelligent, better educated, more likeable, more ambitious, and less tough than either the UFC or the LFC speakers. We had expected this pattern for the traits intelligent, educated, ambitious and tough; but we predicted that Ss would rate Canadian style speakers, particularly the UFC, as more likeable than the SEF speakers. This pattern, however, did not emerge. Quite to the contrary the Ss reacted more favorably to the European style of speech than to their own, a finding which complements the feelings of linguistic insecurity reported earlier. The mean ratings for each of the five adjective traits are as follows.

Trait	F ratio (2, 234 df)	$\overline{X}$ SEF	$\overline{X}$ UFC	$\overline{X}$ LFC
Intelligent	517.64	2.31	3.05	4.30
Educated	7999.99	2.02	3.13	4.95
Ambitious	276.07	3.09	3.68	4.77
Likeable	125.97	2.55	2.76	3.58
Tough	74.58	5.94	5.64	5.15

The next four questions probed the Ss general reactions to the speakers in a manner suggested by Labov (1966, 1967). Once again, we had predicted either significant main effects for speech style or significant occupation-speech style interactions. The Ss generally agreed that the speech style of the SEF speakers was most advantageous ($\overline{X} = 1.90$) followed by that of the UFC ($\overline{X} = 2.84$), and finally the LFC ($\overline{X} = 4.89$). The difference among these means was significant (F = 816.55, df = 2/234, p < .01).

In addition, there was a significant occupation-speech style interaction (F = 3.60, df = 4/234, p < .01) with the workers reacting slightly more favorably toward the LFC style, relative to the students and the workers, than they did toward the SEF or the UFC speakers. Moreover, when asked whether they would consider it personally advantageous to speak like any of the voice samples to which they had listened, the Ss again showed a unanimous preference for the SEF speakers (F = 718.86, df = 2/234, p < .01). The SEF speakers were rated most favorably ($\overline{X} = 2.36$), followed by the UFC ($\overline{X} = 3.30$), and then the LFC ($\overline{X} = 5.57$) speakers. Once again, there was a significant occupation-speech style interaction (F = 5.52, df = 4/234, p < .01). This interaction, shown in Figure 4 indicates that

FIGURE 4. Significant interaction between occupation and speech
style in response to question: Trouvez-vous que ce
serait un avantage pour vous de parler comme lui?

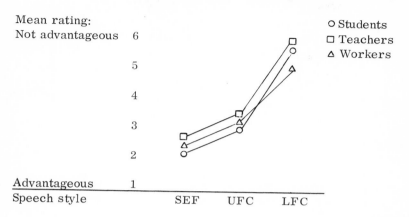

the workers perceived the LFC model to be relatively more favorable
than did the teachers or students. This finding, together with the
similar pattern observed previously suggests that although the workers
view the SEF style of speech as an advantageous model, they feel that
it could be relatively inappropriate in their own occupations. This
finding certainly warrants further investigation.

Responses to the question 'Could this person be a friend of yours?'
showed a significant main effect for speech style (F = 160.11, df =
2/234, p < .01) again pointing up the favorable reaction by all speakers
to the SEF ($\overline{X}$ = 2.78) and UFC ($\overline{X}$ = 2.74) models in contrast to the
LFC model ($\overline{X}$ = 4.00). On this item, the judges made a clear distinction between educated and noneducated speech, but did not react differentially to the SEF and UFC models. The fact that the students
rated the SEF voices less favorably than did either the teachers or
workers, provides a hint that while they admire standard European
French they might not completely accept it or identify with it.

Throughout this research, we have watched for evidence of linguistic insecurity and defensiveness in our Ss while hoping at the
same time to discover whether Quebec style French could emerge as
a symbol of national identity. We believe that we have uncovered a
general malaise with respect to language which might well typify Ss
such as ours who come from predominantly lower-class backgrounds.
It may, however, also derive from the awareness, motivated by past
and present speech improvement movements, that they speak a low
prestige form of the language.

Accompanying this dissatisfaction with the way that they speak, we found a desire for correctness, for norms and for specific information regarding appropriate language usage. As Miner (1939) pointed out, French Canadians have been told for generations that they speak badly and have become apologetic about their speech. But previous speech improvement movements have failed to provide them with any practical means for effecting change. In this respect, we feel that the OLF may well come to play a valuable role in Quebec society although the present lack of objectivity and tendency toward negative value judgments which characterize some of its publications may not be conducive to building a positive self-image in the French Canadian people.

Among the Ss whom we studied, Quebec style speech does not yet appear to serve as a symbol of national identity differentiating French Canadians from other North Americans and also from European speakers of French. We speculated that they might reject SEF as a form of 'cultural imperialism' and show preference for the upper-class French Canadian model. They did not, and the consistent pattern of downgrading both UFC and LFC speech in favor of an SEF style reported by Lambert (1967) and by Brown (1969) again emerged.

While similar tendencies to downgrade their own group have been symptomatic of many minority groups in the United States, we have been unable to find indications of a trend toward an improved self-image comparable to that which has accompanied nationalistic movements among Black and Chicano groups. There are many incidental indications in contemporary Quebec which suggest that French Canadians do indeed have pride in their own language and culture as an entity distinct from that of France. Since the British conquest, they have clung to their language without the benefit of support from France; and a literary tradition distinctly different from that of France has grown up, with some writers choosing 'joual' as the most appropriate medium for expressing the realities of Quebec life (cf. Chantefort 1970). It seems surprising, therefore, that our Ss should indicate so great a willingness to abandon their own traditions and accept those of another cultural group.

A replication of this research, in perhaps five years, when people have had a greater exposure to SEF norms, would be interesting as a test of Labov's hypothesis that subjective evaluation often precedes changes in speech itself (1966). We accept the fact that the findings of this study may not be generalizable to other segments of French Canadian society. Furthermore, we must consider the possibility that our method and techniques did not allow us to assess validly the attitudes of our subjects. People are naturally sensitive about their language; French Canadians at present even more so than others. With these thoughts in mind, we hope to extend the study to other socioeconomic groups and to systematically vary both stimulus and response parameters.

Summary

The picture which emerges clearly from these data suggests an awareness of language variation on the part of French Canadian students, teachers, and workers from three disparate regions of Quebec. Furthermore, these Ss appear aware that there exists some undefined relationship between language and educational, occupational, and social mobility. They view language as a dynamic entity which can nevertheless be influenced by external forces.

The Ss perceive weaknesses in Quebec style French, particularly with respect to its phonology and lexicon; and they regard standard European French as the prestige form of the language. This dissatisfaction with the way that they speak appears to be accompanied by a desire for correctness, for norms, and for specific information regarding appropriate language usage to be supplied, ideally, by Canadians.

The results of this study suggest several important new research directions, and in addition provide baseline data against which to measure the effects of future changes in language policy.

NOTE

[1]We would like to thank Jack F. Griner, Jr., Director of Manufacturing, Frito-Lay Canada Ltd., for allowing us to interview workers in factories under his jurisdiction, and Roger Maréschal of Laval University who provided assistance in locating teachers and students for the study. We are grateful to Fernando Bravo-Ferrer and Réjean Racicot for their sensitivity and diligence in conducting the testing, and to Fred Silny who was responsible for the statistical analysis of the data. This research was supported in part, by grants from the Canada Council and the Defense Research Board to W. E. Lambert and G. R. Tucker.

REFERENCES

Agheyisi, R. and J. A. Fishman. 1970. Language attitude studies: a brief survey of methodological approaches. Anthropological Linguistics. 12.137-57.

Blishen, B. R. 1958. The construction and use of an occupational class scale. Canadian Journal of Economics and Political Science. 24.453-58.

Brown, B. L. 1969. The social psychology of variations in French
Canadian speech styles. Unpublished doctoral dissertation,
McGill University.

Cahiers de l'Office de la langue français, No. I. 1965. Norme de
français écrit et parlé au Québec. Québec, Ministère des Affaires
culturelles au Québec.

Chantefort, P. 1970. Diglossie au Québec: limites et tendances
actuelles. Centre International de Recherches sur le Bilinguisme,
Université Laval.

Charbonneau, R. 1955. Recherche d'une norme phonétique dans la
région de Montréal. In: Etudes sur le parler français au Canada.
Québec.

Chiasson-Lavoie, Michèle and Suzanne Laberge. 1971. Attitudes
face au français parlé à Montréal et degré de conscience de variables linguistiques. Unpublished research paper, McGill University.

Denis, R. 1949. Les vingt siècles du français. Montréal, Fides.
359-77.

Ellis, D. S. 1967. Speech and social status in America. Social
Forces. 45.431-37.

Ellis, P. M. 1965. Les phonèmes du français Maillardvillois.
Canadian Journal of Linguistics. 13.94-98.

Gendron, J. D. 1966. Tendances phonétiques du français parlé au
Canada. Paris, C. Klincksieck.

Giles, H. 1970. Evaluative reactions to accents. Educational Review. 22.211-27.

Halliday, M.A.K. 1968. The users and use of language. In: Readings in the sociology of language. Ed. by J. A. Fishman. The
Hague, Mouton. 139-69.

Harmer, L. C. 1954. The French language today, its characteristics and tendencies. London, Hutchinson.

Labov, W. 1966. The social stratification of English in New York
City. Washington, D. C., Center for Applied Linguistics.

_____. 1967. The effect of social mobility on linguistic behavior.
In: Explorations in sociolinguistics. Ed. by S. Lieberson. The
Hague, Mouton. 58-75.

Lambert, W. E. 1967. A social psychology of bilingualism. Journal of Social Issues. 23.91-109.

Lieberson, S. 1970. Language and ethnic relations in Canada. New
York, Wiley.

Markel, N. N., R. M. Eisler, and H. W. Reese. 1967. Judging
personality from dialect. Journal of Verbal Learning and Verbal
Behavior. 6.33-35.

Miner, H. 1939. St. Denis, a French-Canadian parish. Chicago,
University of Chicago Press.

Pinault, L. and L. Ladouceur. 1971. National language policies. Unpublished undergraduate research paper, McGill University.
Porter, J. 1958. Higher public servants in the bureaucratic elite in Canada. Canadian Journal of Economics and Political Science. 24.483-501.
Royal Commission on Bilingualism and Biculturalism. 1965. (Preliminary report). Ottawa, Queen's Printer.
Spilka, I. V. 1970. For a study of diglossia in French Canada. Unpublished mimeo, Université de Montréal.
Tucker, G. R. 1968. Judging personality from language use: a Filipino example. Philippine Sociological Review. 16.30-39.
Valin, R. 1970. Quel français devons-nous enseigner? In: Cahiers de l'Office de la langue française, No. 7. Québec, Gouvernement du Québec.

SOME 'UNEXPECTED' REACTIONS
TO VARIOUS AMERICAN-ENGLISH DIALECTS[1]

BRUCE FRASER

Boston University

0. Introduction

There is general agreement that the way a person speaks is often coupled--frequently with little or no justification--with a stereotypic level of education, social status, degree of friendliness, and so forth. Advertising agencies have long recognized this and used it effectively. Imagine the red-neck sheriff in the Dodge commercial speaking like Rod Serling. Or imagine Casey Stengel as the doctor on an aspirin commercial. However, we know little at present about the way(s) in which particular features of speech trigger off a certain stereotype in a different speech group.

The experiment reported on here is a modified version of an experiment designed and carried out by Tucker and Lambert, hereafter T-L. (G. Richard Tucker and Wallace E. Lambert, White and negro listeners' reactions to various American-English dialects, Social Forces, 47(4), June 1969.) The purpose of the T-L experiment and ours as well is to indirectly assess the view that one group holds of a second based solely on the recorded speech of the second group.

Described briefly, a sample of 'judges' is asked to listen to a series of taped recordings of different speakers reading a standard passage, and to evaluate relevant personality characteristics of each speaker, using only voice characteristics and speech style as cues. The technique appears to expose the listeners' more private feelings and stereotyped attitudes towards a contrasting group or groups whose language, accent, or dialect is distinctive, and it appears to be reliable in that the same profile of reactions emerges on repeated sampling from a particular social group (T-L, pp. 463-64).

The T-L experiment was developed to answer two questions: are both black and white subjects able to correctly differentiate between dialects; and if so, does any meaningful pattern emerge? The statistical analysis T-L carried out on their data clearly showed that each group of judges differentiates the various dialects, and that some dialect groups were consistently assessed more favorably than others along the various characteristic continua. Our experiment was intended to verify the original T-L results but also to shed light on the following, third, question: does subject judgment of speaker race correlate with his overall evaluation of the speaker?

1. The experiment

1.1 Rating scale. The scales of the T-L experiment were chosen to meet two criteria:

(a) positive ratings should indicate that the listener believes the speakers could attain or have already attained success; and (b) that speakers are 'friendly'. Thus, success should not imply separation from or mobility out of the group represented by the speaker' (T-L, p. 464).

Pilot work with both black and white college students to determine their criteria for both friendship and success as well as two traits (standardness of speech and good upbringing) added by T-L resulted in a set of 15 criteria. They were: Upbringing, Intelligent, Friendly, Educated, Disposition, Speech, Trustworthy, Ambitious, Faith in God, Talented, Character, Determination, Honest, Personality, and Considerate. Each trait could range from 1 to 8 (arbitrarily chosen); for example, an '8' rating for Educated meant that the subject perceived the speaker as highly educated, while a '2' rating for Honest meant that the speaker was perceived as very dishonest. For our experiment, we eliminated six of the T-L traits: Upbringing, Disposition, Faith in God, Character, Personality, and Considerate. This left us with 9 traits which are numbered sequentially in all presentation of our results.

1.2 Stimulus voices. The T-L experiment used recordings of 24 speakers: 4 representatives of 6 dialect groups. The groups were:

(1) Radio announcers (Network speakers)
(2) College-educated white southerners (CEWS speakers)
(3) College-educated black southerners (CEBS speakers)
(4) College-educated black speakers from Mississippi presently attending Howard University in Washington, D. C. (HU speakers)
(5) Southern black students from a small all-black southern college in Mississippi (Miss. Peer)
(6) College-educated black southerners presently living in New York City (NY Alumni)

All speakers in groups 1 and 2 were white; all in groups 3-6 were black. Both male and female speakers were chosen for each group except for the CEWS group which, due to an oversight, contained only male speakers. T-L made two tapes: each consisting of a practice speaker followed by 12 speakers, two speakers from each of the six groups. Each speaker read a passage about English composition (45 seconds approximately) followed by a 30-second pause; the next speaker followed this pause. In our experiment, we used only the T-L tape B which had two female speakers from CEBS, HU, and Miss. Peer groups and two male speakers from the CEWS, Network, and NY Alumni groups. In addition, our version of the B tape omitted the second recording of the passage. It was our conclusion that, because we were using only one tape with a fixed order of speakers, it was important to reduce the overall time of the experiment to maintain interest level so that the later speakers would not systematically suffer in the evaluation.

1.3 Subjects. Subjects were 50 male and female students enrolled in T-60, Child Language, at the Harvard Graduate School of Education, Fall, 1971. Of these subjects, four were black. Of these four, two filled out their evaluation forms with all 4's or 8's, so as to not influence the relative evaluation of the speakers by their white co-students.

1.4 Experimental procedure. The experiment was run in the normal classroom with the 50 subjects plus some auditors and non-subjects. The subjects were asked to listen to the voices on the tape and to rate each speaker from 1-8 in terms of the nine traits listed on the evaluation sheet as well as judge the race of the speaker. A separate rating sheet was provided for the evaluation of each speaker; the order of the traits was the same on each sheet. The practice voice was played, the subjects were asked to make their evaluation in the 30 seconds following, and questions relating to the experimental procedure were then answered. Following that, the modified T-L tape B was played without interruption.

2.0 Results and discussion

2.1 Correspondence to the T-L experiment. The results summarized in Table 1 follow closely the results of the T-L experiment for northern white university students. The mean rating for each group

TABLE 1. Mean ratings and ranks of mean ratings of each group.

Group	Trait										
	Intelligent	Friendly	Educated	Speech	Trustworthy	Ambitious	Talented	Determination	Honest		T-L
	1	2	3	4	5	6	7	8	9	Sum	Sum
Network	6.3	5.4	6.5	6.8	5.2	5.7	5.5	5.7	5.4	14	18
	[1]	[2]	[1]	[1]	[2]	[2]	[1]	[2]	[2]		
CEBS	5.7	5.3	5.6	5.4	5.1	5.9	5.3	6.1	5.1	20	39
	[2]	[3]	[2]	[2]	[3]	[1]	[2]	[1]	[4]		
Howard	5.6	5.5	5.3	5.0	5.5	5.1	5.1	5.2	5.5	24	48
	[3]	[1]	[4]	[4]	[1]	[3]	[3]	[4]	[1]		
CEWS	5.5	5.1	5.5	5.3	4.9	5.1	4.9	5.3	5.0	33	44
	[4]	[4]	[3]	[3]	[4]	[3]	[4]	[3]	[5]		
NY Alum.	5.0	5.3	4.6	4.3	5.1	5.0	4.8	5.1	5.3	38	80
	[5]	[3]	[5]	[5]	[3]	[4]	[5]	[5]	[3]		
Miss. Peer	5.0	5.1	4.5	4.0	5.1	4.8	4.7	5.0	5.3	44	85
	[5]	[4]	[6]	[6]	[3]	[5]	[6]	[6]	[3]		

was computed by taking the mean of all 50 subjects for both speakers of that group. For example, one of the Network speakers had a mean of 5.8 for the trait Trustworthy, the second a rating of 4.5. These two, combined, averaged to 5.2, rounding off (always) to the next highest tenth. The figure 5.2 is what is found in Table 1. The second number in each cell is the ranking for that group for that particular trait. For example, the CEWS group was ranked third for the trait Intelligent. When two groups had the same mean rating, they received the same ranking. For example, the NY Alumni and CEWS groups both had a 5.3 rating for Friendly; they were both ranked third. The column marked 'Sum' is the total, for each group, of the ranking for each trait. The sums, in increasing order, indicate a decreasing overall rating of the groups. The column 'T-L Sum' shows the relative ratings found for the equivalent part of the T-L experiment. (Note: the magnitude of the T-L sums is considerably larger because they were using 15 rather than 9 traits.)

The overall ranking of our experiment and the T-L one is the same with the exception of the reversed order of the HU and CEWS groups. In the T-L case, however, the gap between the Network and CEBS groups was considerably larger: the Network to CEBS ratio of rankings was 18:39 while for our experiment, it was 14:20. Whereas the T-L experiment found the main break between the Network and the CEBS groups, we found it between the CEBS and CEWS groups.

2.2 New results. The most interesting result, however, is presented in Table 2. Leaving aside misjudgments for the Network and Mississippi Peer groups because the percentage is so small, we find the following phenomenon: when the speaker was black, and when subjects misjudged the race of the speaker, they tended, in general, to rate the speaker lower in all categories. There are two exceptions: the Speech of the HU and NY Alumni were rated higher when the speaker was judged white. On the other hand, when the speaker was white (the CEWS group) and when the race of the speaker was misjudged, the subjects did not tend, in general, to rate the speaker lower than the average. (They rated the speakers higher in one, the same in four, and lower in four traits.)

Before drawing any conclusions, it is worth considering whether or not these misjudgers are, on the average, just low evaluators. If this were the case, it would explain the relative lower ratings. Table 3 provides a comparison to the average of the mean ratings of those subjects who missed more than one race identification for those cases where they judged correctly--the Network and Mississippi Peer group.

Table 3 shows that those who misjudged the black speakers did not, in general, rate Network speakers lower than the overall average for each trait. (Four were higher, one the same, four lower.) They did tend to rate the Miss. Peer group lower than the average (except for Speech). However, this lower rating, while approximately equal to that in judging the NY Alumni group when they misjudged the race, was nowhere as great as in the CEBS or HU groups, when they also misjudged race.

What, then, explains the data in Table 2? Although there are many hypotheses compatible with the results, the following strikes me as an explanation worth consideration. Assume that for every dialect group, however such a group is to be ultimately defined, has developed a stereotypic pairing function which maps each point on a scale called 'Manner of Speaking' (linguistic features such as pronunciation,

TABLE 2. Comparison of mean ratings for those who misjudged race to the mean ratings for all subjects.

Group	Trait									% Wrong race	T-L % Wrong race
	Intelligent 1	Friendly 2	Educated 3	Speech 4	Trustworthy 5	Ambitious 6	Talented 7	Determination 8	Honest 9		
Network	6.3	5.4	6.5	6.8	5.2	5.7	5.5	5.7	5.4	1%B*	5%B
	---	---	---	---	---	---	---	---	---	---	
CEBS	5.7	5.3	5.6	5.4	5.1	5.9	5.3	6.1	5.1	28%W	51%W
	4.8	5.0	4.8	5.1	4.7	5.3	4.3	5.5	4.9		
Howard	5.6	5.5	5.3	5.0	5.5	5.1	5.1	5.2	5.5	10%W	14%W
	4.9	4.8	5.0	5.2	4.8	4.3	4.0	4.3	4.3		
CEWS	5.5	5.1	5.5	5.3	4.9	5.1	4.9	5.3	5.0	12%B	13%B
	5.5	4.8	5.5	5.3	4.6	5.1	5.1	5.1	4.6		
NY Alum.	5.0	5.3	4.6	4.3	5.1	5.0	4.8	5.1	5.3	40%W	51%W
	4.8	5.1	4.4	4.4	5.0	4.9	4.7	5.0	5.2		
Miss. Peer	5.0	5.1	4.5	4.0	5.1	4.8	4.7	5.0	5.3	5%W	6%W
	4.5	4.5	4.3	4.0	4.3	4.3	4.4	4.5	4.5		

syntactic form, choice of words, intonation, rate of speech, voice quality, and so forth) onto a scale for certain character traits, for example, those used in the experiment. For example, the dialect group represented by large northern university graduate students might pair a high degree of 'standardness' of speech (that of the Network group) with a high degree of education but a less high degree of trust. And so forth. Now assume that this pairing is race-dependent. That is, given a level of speech the pairing has one set of values for white speakers, for example, but another for black speakers. If, for a given manner of speaking, this pairing showed higher values for black as opposed to white speakers, this would account for the data in Tables 2 and 3. Stated another way, it wasn't that the misjudgers

TABLE 3. Comparison of mean ratings for subjects who misjudged race to overall mean ratings for Network and
Mississippi peer groups.

Group	Traits								
	Intelligent	Friendly	Educated	Speech	Trustworthy	Ambitious	Talented	Determination	Honest
	1	2	3	4	5	6	7	8	9
Network									
Overall mean	6.3	5.4	6.5	6.8	5.2	5.7	5.5	5.7	5.4
Misjudgers' mean	6.2	5.6	6.3	6.7	5.3	5.5	5.5	5.9	5.5
Deviation	-.1	+.2	-.2	-.1	+.1	-.2	.0	+.2	+.1
Miss. Peer									
Overall mean	5.0	5.1	4.5	4.0	5.1	4.8	4.7	5.0	5.3
Misjudgers' mean	4.7	5.0	4.4	4.2	4.9	4.5	4.4	4.8	5.1
Deviation	-.3	-.1	-.1	+.2	-.2	-.3	-.3	-.2	-.2

in the experiment were rating low, but that the correct judgers were
rating high. This explanation also accounts for the fact that those who
misjudged the race for the CEBS, HU, and NY Alumni groups (cf.
Table 2) rated the Speech the same or higher than the overall average
while rating other traits lower.

3. Conclusion

It is not surprising that the subject group of university graduate
students systematically ranked the dialect groups as in the T-L
experiment, nor that they characteristically misjudged the race of
the CEBS, HU, or NY Alumni groups. What is interesting is the extent to which the rating seems affected by the perceived race of the
speaker.

Before one exclaims that here is yet another form of covert
racism, I suggest that this phenomenon is hardly rare. We will
surely find the same sort of scale-sliding across wide ranges of

ethnic groups, regional groups, and, if made obvious, across religious groups. The simple fact is that people will judge differentially on the basis of certain cues--in this case speech alone--because
of their experience and certain, albeit inaccurate, stereotypes. No
amount of research and breast beating is going to erase these stereotypes, at least in the foreseeable future. However, I suggest that
research along the lines discussed above can and should be used to
make various (dialect) groups aware of what stereotypes they hold
and the ways in which they view other groups, so that they may take
steps to counteract this attitude when it is clearly beside the point.

NOTE

[1] The work reported here was supported in part by Ford Foundation
Grant No. 700-0656 to the Language Research Foundation. I would
like to thank Richard Tucker for making available his tapes of dialect speakers to me, and Mary Selkirk for her valuable assistance in
calculating the results.

ATTITUDES AND LEARNING
A SECOND LANGUAGE

JOHN MACNAMARA

McGill University

Disagreement between teachers and psychologists I find easy to cope with, because I usually agree with the teachers. Agreement between them is another matter, and in this paper I have to deal with it. They both agree that favorable attitudes are vital for success in language learning and further that a favorable attitude is one of the major contributors to success in language learning. I am going to throw caution to the winds and argue that both teachers and psychologists are mistaken, that favorable attitudes are of only minor importance.

For years I held the majority view on attitudes. In Ireland, sensible people maintained that children from English-speaking homes (at least 97% of the population) learned little Irish in school because parents did not foster favorable attitudes to Irish. By this they meant that parents failed to communicate to children a sense of the historic and cultural value of the language and a pride in its role as a symbol of nationhood; they may also have meant that some parents went so far as to speak disparagingly of Irish. People who were even more sensible attributed the weakness of Irish in the schools to the fact that in Ireland adults manage very well without knowing Irish, and children somehow notice this. My colleague, Professor Wallace Lambert (1967), makes a distinction, which almost captures the two Irish views, between what he calls an 'integrative' and an 'instrumental' attitude to language learning, an integrative attitude being a desire to know and become friendly with speakers of a language, an instrumental one being a desire to better oneself materially by means of the language. He adduces evidence that an integrative attitude is more likely to lead to success than an instrumental one.

In his book, Foreign language learning, Leon Jakobovits (1970) is somewhat embarrassed by the research findings in the area which either fail to show a correlation between measured attitudes and measured attainments in language courses, or show a low one. In his summing up he seems to lay aside the research and talks instead about what he considers to be the important role of attitudes. He is also exercised by the finding that many students in foreign language classes do not want to be there; apart from considerations of human dignity and liberty, he feels that such overall attitudes augur badly for the success of their work.

My new scepticism comes from several quarters, not least of which is the realization that historically, language shifts have generally been accompanied by unfavorable attitudes to the conquering people and their language. There has always been some antipathy of Irish people to England and English; yet English replaced Irish. The highland Scots behaved just like the Irish, and while the Welsh proved tougher than either, they too seem to be in the process of changing to English. They are, of course, following in ancient footsteps, because centuries ago the celtic languages of Europe succumbed to Latin. Despite determined efforts to prevent it, the people of Provence have accepted French in place of Provencal, and the Catalonians have learned Castillian in addition to Catalan. But there is no need to multiply examples (as long as we recognize the possibilities for multiplication!).

No doubt the thought has occurred to many readers that the historical argument is somewhat specious as it stands, since a people like the Irish might well combine an unfavorable integrative attitude to the English with a positive instrumental one. Undoubtedly they did, and even though an instrumental attitude is the less effective of the two according to Professor Lambert, one could still account for the language switch in terms of attitude. But to leave it at that is, I think, to miss the dynamics of language learning.

A child suddenly transported from Toronto to Berlin will rapidly learn German no matter what he thinks of the Germans. Indeed when he makes his first appearance on the street and meets German children he is likely to be appalled by the experience. They will not understand a word he says; they will not make sense when they speak; and they are likely to punish him severely by keeping him incommunicado. I have argued elsewhere (Macnamara 1971a, 1972) that he will learn German because he must understand what is being said to him precisely when it is said, and he must communicate precisely when the need arises. I do not believe that he learns German because of an appreciation that German will prove useful at some future date, but rather because it is useful now. This is not what Professor Lambert or Professor Jakobovits had in mind when they spoke of attitudes or motivation; this is not what people generally have in mind when they speak of language learning in classrooms. I suspect that the historical facts can be explained along similar lines: the Irish, for example, learned English in situations where they had to use it. Curiously, the Irish learned English for the most part at a time when schooling was outlawed for Catholics, who were the overwhelming majority of the population (see Macnamara 1971).

It would be obtuse to attribute linguistic attitudes to babies who are learning their mother tongue. They need to understand what is said to them and to express their wants and feelings; they even like to talk for the sake of talking and to engage in language games; but they hardly see far enough ahead or deeply enough into history to form what educationalists and psychologists call attitudes to language. Yet of all language learners they are the model. If babies manage without such attitudes, the likelihood is that adolescents and adults do too, at least to the extent to which they are successful. The only part that I see for long term attitudes in older people is that they might influence their approach to opportunities for using the second language.

I want to carry this analysis further and apply it to the school; but before I do, I want to clear up one theoretical point. Many people imagine that babies learn languages in a special manner which is different from the way older persons learn them. The magic facility which enables babies to just pick up their mother tongue disappears, they say, and then it is the hard grind of vocabulary and grammar lessons. They miss the obvious point that for an adult to know a language is in all essentials the same as for a baby to know it. Since the product of the learning process is the same, the simplest and most parsimonious hypothesis is that the learning process too is the same. Suits which look identical are probably cut from the same pattern. Moreover language is much too complex to permit of its being taught explicitly. Whatever we think about the psychological reality of transformational grammars, at least the study of them has enlarged our imaginations, and we now realize that the specifications for any language would look more like some massive computer program than a traditional grammar book. There is, then, just as much magic in an adult's learning a language as in a child's doing so.

The theoretical confusions that I have dealt with so far are as nothing compared with those which exist in the classroom. Teacher and children wallow in what must be the nearest thing to total misunderstanding, and it has to do with basic attitudes. The teacher believes that language is to be respected and caressed for its own sake, that one needs to do penance and prepare oneself to capture the fine points of pronunciation and grammar as Sir Galahad prepared himself to seek the Holy Grail. Children are simply stunned by this attitude. They believe that language is for communicating; they see it as a modest tool, but communication is what it is all about. I believe the children are right and the teachers wrong. I also believe that the only way to make the linguistic magic work is to become vitally engaged in communicating.

I can demonstrate the confusion more strikingly, if I contrast babies learning language with children in classrooms. Babies begin with one-word sentences and manage to communicate very well in them. School children are usually required to speak in full sentences in an unnatural manner: <u>that is not a hen; that is a lawn-mower</u>. The teacher sees a virtue in full sentences; the baby is interested only in communicating.

The baby gets away with one-word sentences because his mother guesses his meaning just as he guesses hers. I have argued elsewhere (Macnamara 1972) that to guess meaning is one of the essential strategies of language learning. In the classroom the only guess that the child makes is that the teacher has nothing to say to him, and he for his part has nothing to tell the teacher. The child's mind is turned off. And since the teacher always knows the answer before he puts a question, there is only an appearance of conversation. It is like a very dull Chekov play: everyone talks, but nobody really listens. Again, the teacher sees talking as a valuable exercise, and the child regards it as nonsense.

A mother accepts all the child's remarks which are both true and mannerly; she does not often correct pronunciation or grammar until the child is about five by which time he is almost a master of his language. The conscientious teacher pounces on all departures from phonological and syntactic perfection; she does not care what the child says as long as he says it correctly. The schoolchild, unused to such treatment in learning his first language, is unnerved and finds himself at a disadvantage. He does not, of course, analyze the situation; he merely becomes bored or concludes that he lacks talent for languages.

Finally, a mother does not have another language in which to talk to the baby if he fails to understand what she says. She has to make do with gestures, facial expressions, and exaggerated tones of voice. Because they are both involved in communicating they usually manage somehow. How different it is in the classroom! Teacher and child usually have another common language, which means that they could communicate much better if they really needed to. Indeed they often do have recourse to the other language. Teachers, unlike mothers, do not exploit gestures, intonation, facial expressions, and events in the environment to provide the child with clues which will guide him to the meaning. The result is that classroom conversations seem remote, unreal, and often lifeless compared with the conversations of a mother and child. Basically it is the same disease that we have encountered before: the teacher sees language mainly as something to be learned; the child sees it mainly as a means of communication. He is seldom interested in language, but rather in the information which it conveys.

Babies do not differ much in ability to learn a language. Leave aside the deaf ones and those who are severely handicapped mentally and the rest seem to learn with little difficulty. One may be a little more talkative than another; one may progress a little quicker than another and learn a larger vocabulary. But we must look closely if we are to notice the differences. In the essentials there is little individual variation. In foreign language classrooms the variation is enormous, and this I take as a sign of failure to engage the children's faculté de langage. I am not surprised to find enormous differences among people skiing, but I would be if I were to find them among people walking. Walking is 'natural' whereas skiing is somehow 'artificial'. It would seem that homes, and streets, produce 'natural' language whereas schools produce 'artificial' language, and that the variation among students is an indication of the artificiality. Our task is to make the school more like the home and the street. If my analysis is correct, this means among other things that we must stop talking about attitudes and talk much more about communicating. My belief is that when we really learn this lesson, individual differences in linguistic attainment will cease to be noticeable. I also forecast a lean time for those whose business it is to predict such differences.

REFERENCES

Jakobovits, Leon A. 1970. Foreign language learning. Rowley, Massachusetts, Newbury House.

Lambert, Wallace E. 1967. A social psychology of bilingualism. Journal of Social Issues. 23.91–109.

Macnamara, John. 1971a. Successes and failures in the movement for the restoration of Irish. In: Can language be planned? Ed. by Joan Rubin and Bjorn H. Jernudd. University of Hawaii Press. 65–94.

_____. 1971b. The cognitive strategies of language learning. Paper read at Conference on Child Language, Chicago.

_____. 1972. Cognitive basis of language learning in infants. Psychological Review. 1–13.

A PRELIMINARY REPORT ON A STUDY OF THE LINGUISTIC CORRELATES OF RATERS' SUBJECTIVE JUDGMENTS OF NON-NATIVE ENGLISH SPEECH

LESLIE A. PALMER

Georgetown University

Recent sociolinguistic studies suggest that the evaluation which a listener is likely to give to an individual's speech will depend heavily upon his previously formed attitudes toward the dialect, social class, and ethnic group membership of that speaker. Even when listeners cannot depend upon visual cues, they are able with considerable consistency to identify the social status and ethnicity of speakers (Harms 1963, Shuy 1969). Language quite obviously reveals much about a speaker's status even to the nonlinguistically trained listener, but not very much is yet known about what specific language and nonlanguage cues affect the listener's judgments.

Lambert and his colleagues (Lambert 1960, Anisfeld and Lambert 1964) have shown that subjective evaluations of speech are systematically affected by associations made with stereotypes held about majority and minority groups. Labov (1966) on the other hand has been concerned with the identification of specific language variables with certain social classes. Williams (1970) in an attempt to relate the findings of the two different approaches called for research 'to link whatever language and speech features serve as salient cues in this judgmental process with whatever kinds of evaluations or stereotypes are of interest to us in the behavior of listeners'. Of particular interest to the current study is the fact that he was able to reliably predict both status and judgment ratings from certain selected

41

language features. Prominent among these were silent pausing, main verb construction, and the pronunciation of certain sounds.

The sociolinguist is correctly concerned with the social implications of the 'different' speech of minority groups and social classes. In the research cited, the subjects all belonged to quite well defined, stable groups but there is another more transient group for whom the reactions of the majority population are quite critical. This is the group of adult, non-native English speakers who are in the United States for relatively short periods of time during which they must use the English language effectively to gain maximum benefit from their cultural and educational experience. As Richards (1971) points out, if a foreign speaker deviates very far from the grammatical and/or phonological norms of the English-speaking community, he may elicit unfavorable reactions. What characterizes unacceptable non-native speech is unknown, however. Richards suggests that research similar to that being done by sociolinguists on other groups be done on evaluative reactions to foreign speech.

This group of non-native speakers differs in several respects from the groups usually studied by sociolinguists. They are not a stable group within a limited geographical area as are most dialect speakers. The English they speak is not characteristic of any known American English dialect. [1] What is of even greater importance is that they do not all have the same competence in English. This means that it is exceedingly difficult to determine the extent to which reactions to their speech are based on associations with stereotypes about 'foreigners' or 'funny English', for example, and how much is based on their actual language performance.

In view of the lack of work with this particular group and the general interest in the problems of relating subjective evaluations of speech to specific linguistic data the following study was undertaken. Its primary goal is to investigate the relationship between natives' subjective judgments of non-native speech samples and linguistic (and extralinguistic) cues which affected those judgments. Questions for which answers are being sought are as follow.

(1) What are the important cues in the subjects' recorded speech which affect the judges' evaluations ?
   (a) Is rate of speech an important variable affecting judges' ratings ?
   (b) Are kind and frequency of hesitation phenomena highly correlated with judges' ratings ?
   (c) Is accuracy of pronunciation a major variable ?
   (d) Are grammatical correctness and complexity important variables ?

    (e) Are there interactions among the above factors which significantly affect the judges' ratings?

(2) Are the important cues the same for subjects with different native language backgrounds?

(3) Can the judges, upon questioning, specify the linguistic cues on which they presumably based their ratings?

(4) Will the judges' subjective evaluations of the subjects' personal characteristics correlate with their language ratings?

(5) Will the judges react differentially to the speech samples because of the subjects' native language backgrounds? For example, will the judges systematically rate Vietnamese lower than Spanish speakers, etc.?

(6) Can judges consistently identify the native language background of the subjects?

(7) Can untrained, linguistically naive judges reliably rate samples of non-native English speech?

(8) Will the judges' ratings correlate highly with the subjects' scores on standard English proficiency tests?

For this study, data are generated from four sources: (1) subjective ratings of speech performances, (2) judges' commentaries on their ratings, (3) judges' responses to the items on questionnaires, and (4) linguistic analyses of the subjects' language performances. Collection has been completed on the first three; the analyses required for the fourth have only just been started.

Subjects

The Subjects (Ss) chosen for the study came from four unrelated language backgrounds: Arabic, Lingala, Spanish, and Vietnamese.[2] All were adults (average age 32.5 years) in professional or semi-professional fields, studying English at Georgetown University prior to beginning academic studies in other U.S. colleges and universities. From among the 50 Ss recorded, 36 were selected for the study, 9 each from the 4 language backgrounds. Of this total, only 3 were women. As measured by standard tests of English proficiency, each group of 9 ranged from 'poor' to 'excellent' in English ability.

Respondents

The Respondents (Rs) were all student volunteers from Georgetown University. All those interested in participating in the project filled out a two-page questionnaire which included questions about travel and residence abroad, and years of study and degree of proficiency in foreign languages. Questions were also asked regarding teaching

and evaluation experience. Based largely on answers to these questions a selection was made of eighteen Rs who had minimum experience with foreign languages. None had regularly taught any language
including English as a foreign language; none had spent an extended
period abroad in the countries or areas of the world in which the S's
languages were spoken; and none were bilinguals. Three were males
and fifteen were females. Their average age was twenty-one years.
Rs who had been teachers of English or who had training in the field
of linguistics were eliminated for two reasons. First, an inexperienced group of judges would more closely approximate the general
population and second, the writer's experience in using trained linguists for oral rating tasks had been discouraging (cf. Briere 1967).

Recording procedure

Each S was recorded individually by an experienced interviewer.
At the beginning of the recording session, he was told that his recording was to be used in a study of the special problems which speakers
of different foreign languages had with English and that such a study
would enable the staff to develop better teaching materials. To put
him at ease, the S was assured that his recording was not a test of
how well he was performing in his class. In many cases, Ss expressed pleasure in being able to contribute to the study. Following
a brief explanation of the procedure to be followed the first task was
presented.

Task A: reading. The S was given a copy of a brief (250 word)
description of an unusual celebration held in the Shetland Islands. He
was asked to read the text silently as the interviewer read it aloud to
him. Then, after a brief pause, the interviewer asked the S to read
the text aloud for recording. The average reading time was 2.4
minutes.

Task B: retelling. The interviewer informed the S that the next
task would be to retell what he had just read in his own words. Before
starting, however, he was given one to two minutes to re-read the
text. Then the text was removed, the recorder started, and the S
retold what he had read as best he could. No prompting of any sort
was given by the interviewer. The average retelling time was 2.2
minutes.

Task C: interview. At the completion of Task B, the recorder
was left on and the interviewer discussed the subject of the text with
the S. As the discussion continued, the interviewer directed the

discussion away from the written text to some holiday or festival celebrated in the S's country and through questions helped the S to develop a description of that event.

Task D: narration. As the final task, the S was asked to tell about the particular holiday or celebration from his own country which he and the interviewer had discussed. The average time for the narration was 2.4 minutes. The average time for completing all four tasks was 25 minutes.

There were several purposes for setting up this particular sequence of tasks.

(1) Since several samples of speech were required it seemed more desirable to have these related in some meaningful way than to collect three or four unrelated samples.

(2) It was felt that this particular sequence of tasks would lead each S from a maximally controlled situation (reading) to an essentially free situation (narration) but that even the last task would be more comparable from S to S than it would in most other types of interview situations. The judges then could rate the Ss performance on essentially comparable tasks which should help raise the reliability of their evaluations.

(3) It seemed quite possible that there would be fewer failures to perform all four tasks in such a structured situation and it was thought necessary to get complete sets for all Ss included in the study.

Rating procedure: subjective

Because the interview, Task C, had both the S's and the interviewer's voices on tape, it was excluded from the evaluation procedure. For each of the other three tasks, the recorded tape segments were randomized and test tapes comprised of four segments each were assembled. Since each of the Ss was to be rated twice on each task, the thirty-six segments for each task appeared once in each of two random orders. No recording was edited or modified in any way. Each R evaluated a total of twelve tape segments, four at each of three sessions scheduled two to three days apart. Only one task was judged at each session and the order in which the tasks were judged was D, A, B. They were evaluated on a 5-point scale where 1 was low and 5 was high. Therefore each S was judged six times, two for each task yielding task ratings ranging from 2 to 10 and total ratings on all three tasks ranging from 6 to 30. The average time for completing all three sets of ratings was about three hours.

The procedure followed for each rating session is briefly outlined as follows.[3]

(1) The R listened to a training tape with four speakers performing the task to be judged and then assigned ratings to each performance. He could replay the training tape at any time during the rating session.

(2) The R listened to the first test tape segment, replayed as often as he wished and then assigned a rating. He recorded the number of times he listened to the tape on the rating form. Then he wrote comments about why he gave the rating he did.

(3) The R repeated Step 2 for each of the other three test tape segments.

(4) The rating sheets were removed and the R was asked to complete a questionnaire for each of the four tapes rated. The test tapes could be replayed again if the R wished to do so.

(5) The R was asked not to discuss the experiment or his experience as a rater with any of his fellow students.

Rating procedure: analytic

To answer the linguistic questions posed, the recorded speech samples will be analyzed for: (1) accuracy of stress and intonation, (2) accuracy of pronunciation, (3) kind and frequency of hesitation phenomena, (4) types of grammatical errors, and (5) grammatical complexity. To avoid circularity the analysis will be done by two trained linguists working independently. The results of these analyses will then be compared with the subjective ratings, the Respondents' comments about their ratings, and the questionnaire data. An attempt will be made to predict the speech ratings from the results of the linguistic analyses and the questionnaire data to determine what combination of factors significantly affected the R's evaluations.

Some preliminary results

The subjective evaluations have been completed and some preliminary analysis has been done on the data. The analysis of the speech samples has just gotten underway so that the following results are based only on the analysis of the ratings and questionnaire data.

A question critical to the success of the study is whether the linguistically unsophisticated judges could rate the speech samples reliably. If they could not, little possibility exists for relating results of subsequent linguistic analyses to the subjective ratings in any meaningful way. Fortunately the Rs were quite consistent in their judgments as indicated in Tables 1 and 2.

TABLE 1. Reliability of ratings for tasks across languages.

Task	r_{11}
A (reading)	.83
B (retelling)	.74
C (narration)	.75

TABLE 2. Reliability of ratings by language background across tasks.

Language	r_{11}
Lingala	.80
Arabic	.79
Vietnamese	.79
Spanish	.64

These reliability coefficients are considerably higher than those often found for judges' ratings of foreign speech. The expected reliability coefficient would be .4 or .5.

Not a central question to this study but one that does relate to the question of reactions to stereotypes is whether the Rs could correctly identify the native language of the Ss from the recorded speech samples. To eliminate possible clues from the Ss topics, the Rs were asked to identify L_1 from the recorded readings (Task A). They were also asked to indicate which areas of the world they thought the Ss came from: Africa (sub-Sahara), Latin America, Middle East/North Africa, Southeast Asia, Europe. They were not told, however, that the Ss were from different world areas and L_1 backgrounds. With the exception of the Ss who spoke Spanish, the Rs were not very successful at identifying native language background.

An interesting observation is that there were only two instances where speakers' L_1 backgrounds were correctly identified by both judges. The two speakers were from Spanish-speaking countries. Because the Ss' recordings were assembled in random orders, most test tapes had two (rarely three) speakers from the same L_1. It is curious, however, that Rs invariably failed to recognize Ss from the same language background. This was true even for the Spanish speakers which the Rs correctly identified most often. It is possible that each R expected to rate four different L_1 speakers and so

TABLE 3.

Ss language	Percent guessed correctly		Other languages guessed
	Area	Language	
Spanish	77*	56	Turkish, Lebanese, French, Russian, Arabic, Swedish, Italian
Arabic	33	31	Afrikaans, Korean, Czech, Indian (3), Chinese (2), Tibetan, (Nigerian), Spanish
Vietnamese	44	20	Indian (2), Japanese, Thai, French (3), German, Chinese, Swedish, Arabic, Hebrew
Lingala	22	12**	Spanish (5), Hindu, Persian, Indian, Turkish, Arabic (3), Vietnamese (2)

*Both Europe and Latin America were accepted as correct choices.
**Guesses of 'Congo' and 'Swahili' were accepted.

rejected the possibility of finding more than one S from the same background. It also seems possible that particular foreign English speech, e. g. Spanish, is not so distinctive as one is led to believe.

A more interesting question is whether judges react differentially to speech samples of Ss from different L_1 backgrounds. An affirmative answer could presumably indicate reactions associated with stereotypes about particular foreigners, e. g. the Oriental or the Spanish speaker. However, such a finding is not possible here because (1) the Rs generally were not successful in correctly identifying the L_1 of the Ss, and (2) the English language ability of the Ss varied. Unfortunately there is no reliable means of judging whether speakers have equal ability in L_2. Therefore it is impossible to determine the extent to which variance might be caused by negative or positive reactions to stereotypes and the extent to which it is caused by differences in L_2 ability. The question is moot.

It is interesting to note, however, that the rater reliability for the Spanish speakers was markedly lower than for the other three language groups. This suggests that the Rs may have treated the Spanish Ss somewhat differently. However, the difference was not significant beyond the 20% level (p < .20). An inspection of the ratings of Ss wrongly identified as Spanish (Lingala - 5; Arabic - 1) uncovered nothing.

An analysis of variance which was run on the ratings indicated a significant difference (p < .05) in performance between language groups but showed no significant difference (p < .25) in the difficulty of the tasks. The latter finding is to be expected since each task was judged independently and the score distributions were normalized because of the scoring method. The interaction between rater and task was unexpectedly nonsignificant; the F-ratio was less than 1. Ironically, the answer to the question of differential response to Ss of different L_1 backgrounds can be yes but the reasons why remain obscure.

An assumption made by many test users is that there is a high positive correlation between ability to speak and L_2 and ability to perform on auditory and written proficiency tests in L_2. The ALI/GU English proficiency tests were used only to select Ss who might be roughly comparable in English ability but since the data were available, correlations were run between the test scores and the Rs' ratings.

TABLE 4. Correlations between ALI/GU test scores and task ratings.

Task	r
A	.29
B	.29
D	-.07
Total A+B+D	.25

The correlations between the ratings on the tasks and the Ss' ALI/GU test scores was lower than expected. Past studies comparing interview ratings with test scores have shown correlations in the .4 to .6 range.

TABLE 5.   Correlations between ALI/GU test scores and ratings by language groups.

Language	r
Lingala	.87
Spanish	.46
Arabic	-.001
Vietnamese	-.04

Though one's eye is caught by the wide disparity in the correlations, it is not safe because the numbers are so small (N=9) to speculate about the reasons why, for example, the r is so high for Lingala speakers. Considering both tables, however, one is tempted to conclude that speaking ability may not be measured to any substantial degree by multiple-choice auditory and grammar tests.

In face-to-face interviews, the Ss' personality and appearance often affect the judges' ratings either positively or negatively. To an extent, this personal factor is removed when the evaluation is done using a tape recording. However, definite impressions are formed about the speaker and it seemed quite likely that these impressions would markedly affect the Rs' judgments.

A factor analysis was run on the data generated by the ratings and the questionnaires. The program gave 34 factors for 36 variables; eight factors were rotated. Two of these seem to load on 'personal characteristics' of the speakers. One, which identifies with Task B, also loads on the Task B ratings as one would expect. The other, which is determined largely by the D_2 and D_4 questionnaire scales, does not load on the task D ratings. This suggests that the language judgments for the 'narration' may have been made quite independently of the Rs' evaluations of the Ss' personal characteristics. This is an extremely interesting finding which runs counter to intuitive assumptions about the effects of speakers' personalities upon evaluative judgments. Further investigation is being done.

As stated earlier, this paper is a preliminary report only. Answers to the more interesting linguistic questions await completion of the analyses currently underway.

NOTES

[1]A distinction is made here between English as a foreign language and English as a second language. Puerto Ricans, Mexicans, Chinese, and other ethnic groups living in relatively permanent communities in the U. S. are presumed to be speakers of ESL and so are excluded from consideration here.

[2]The reasons for choosing Ss from these particular language backgrounds were (1) convenience--the required number were available; and (2) curiosity--perhaps judges would respond quite differently to speakers from widely different language backgrounds.

[3]For specific details about the raters' instructions and the questionnaires, see the Appendix.

REFERENCES

Anisfeld, M., N. Bogo, and W. E. Lambert. 1962. Evaluational reactions to accented English speech. Journal of Abnormal and Social Psychology. 65.223-31.

Briere, Eugene J. 1967. Phonological testing reconsidered. Language Learning. 17.163-71.

Carroll, Brendan J. 1963. Speech intelligibility--a psycholinguistic study. Unpublished doctoral dissertation, Edinburgh.

Carroll, John B. 1961. Fundamental considerations in testing for English language proficiency of foreign students. Testing the English Proficiency of Foreign Students. Washington, D.C., Center for Applied Linguistics. 30-40.

Catford, J. C. 1950. Intelligibility. English Language Teaching. 5(1).7-15.

Chafe, Wallace L. 1970. Meaning and the structure of language. Chicago, The University of Chicago Press.

Chomsky, Noam. 1965. Aspects of the theory of syntax. Cambridge, MIT Press.

Erwin-Tripp, Susan. 1964. An analysis of the interaction of language, topic and listener. American Anthropologist (Special Publication) 66(6).86-102.

Godshalk, Fred I., Frances Swineford, and William E. Coffman. 1966. The measurement of writing ability. New York, College Entrance Examination Board.

Harms, L. S. 1963. Status cues in speech: extra-race and extra-region identification. Lingua. 12.300-06.

_____. 1961. Listener comprehension of speakers of three status groups. Language and Speech. 4.109-12.

Harris, David P. 1969. Testing English as a second language. New York, McGraw-Hill.

Jakobovits, Leon A. 1970. Foreign language learning: a psycholinguistic analysis of the issues. Rowley, Mass., Newbury House Publishers.

Katz, J. J., and P. M. Postal. 1964. An integrated theory of linguistic descriptions. Cambridge, Mass., MIT Press.

Labov, W. 1966. The social stratification of English in New York City. Washington, D.C., Center for Applied Linguistics.

Lado, Robert. 1962. Language testing: the construction and use of foreign language tests. New York, McGraw-Hill.

Lambert, W. E., R. C. Hodgson, R. C. Gardner, and S. Fillenbaum. 1960. Evaluational reactions to spoken languages. Journal of Abnormal and Social Psychology. 60.44-51.

Maclay, H. and C. E. Osgood. 1959. Hesitation phenomena in spontaneous English speech. Word. 15.19-44.

Oller, John W., Jr. 1969. Language communication and second language learning. Unpublished.

Pitcher, Barbara and B. Jung. 1967. Ra with David P. Harris and Leslie A. Palmer. The relation between scores on the test of English as a foreign language and ratings of actual theme writing. Statistical report SR-67-9. Princeton, Educational Testing Service.

Rice, Frank A. 1959. The Foreign Service Institute tests of language proficiency. The Linguistic Reporter. 1(2).4.

Richards, J. C. 1971. Error analysis and second language strategies. Language Sciences. 17.12-22

Shuy, R. W. 1969. Subjective judgments in sociolinguistic analysis. Monograph Series on Languages and Linguistics. Ed. by J. E. Alatis. 22.175-85.

Spolsky, Bernard. 1968. What does it mean to know a language or how do you perform your competence. Unpublished.

_____. 1969. Reduced redundancy as a language testing tool. Unpublished.

Upshur, John A. 1968. Measurement of oral communication. Unpublished.

Von Raffler-Engel, W. and C. K. Sigelman. 1971. Rhythm, narration, description in the speech of black and white school children. Language Sciences. 18.9-14.

Williams, F. 1970. Psychological correlates of speech characteristics: on sounding 'disadvantaged'. Journal of Speech and Hearing Research. 13.472-88.

APPENDIX

It is probably safe to say that every country in the world has its own holidays and celebrations. Some of these are national holidays, such as Independence Day or New Year's Day. But other celebrations are held in just one region of the country. Often they celebrate local events which took place many, many years ago.

In Great Britain, one of the most unusual local celebrations is held in a small town in the Shetland Islands--the islands which form the most northern part of the British Isles. For many centuries these islands were occupied by the Vikings, the bold sailors from Norway and Denmark who attacked many parts of Europe in the 9th and 10th centuries. It seems very likely that this special celebration was begun by the Vikings when they lived on these islands.

The celebration takes place every year on the last Tuesday in January. Its purpose is to celebrate the end of the coldest and darkest part of the winter. After this date the days will begin to get longer, and the sun will begin to grow warmer. One can understand why the people want to celebrate this event!

To prepare for their celebration, the people build a huge boat which looks just like the ones the Vikings once used. Then, on the night of the celebration, a huge crowd of people marches down to the boat. They are led by several men who are dressed like Viking sailors. The boat is then dragged through the streets of the town, accompanied by the music of bands. All the people carry burning torches.

After the boat has been pulled through the town, it is taken down to the water. The people then throw their lighted torches into the boat, which burns with a great fire. This is the sign for parties to begin, and the people go to their homes to dance, sing, and eat until morning.

RATING SHEET FOR TRAINING TAPES

Rating Scale:	5 - high
	4
	3 - mid
	2
	1 - low

Rater Code:____

Tape Number:_____   Rating:_____

Tape Number:_____   Rating:_____

Tape Number:_____   Rating:_____

Tape Number:_____   Rating:_____

DIRECTIONS FOR RATING TAPE SEGMENTS 'A'

Task   In this part of the experiment, you will rate how well some non-native speakers read a short prose passage in English.

Rating Training Tapes

First, listen to all four speakers on the Training Tape. Then replay the tape and rate the speakers' performances using the 5-point scale shown on the 'Rating Sheet'.

Rating Test Tapes

(1) After you have rated the speakers on the training tape, listen to the first speaker on the Test Tape. DO NOT STOP THE TAPE UNTIL HE HAS FINISHED SPEAKING. You may then replay the tape segment as many times as you wish before you decide on your rating. It is important, however, that you indicate on the 'Subject Rating Sheet' the number of times you replayed this segment. As you listen, you may want to take notes about the speaker's performance to help you decide on your rating. For these notes, use the separate note paper provided for this purpose.

(2) When you have decided on the rating, put it on the 'Subject Rating Sheet' and then make any comments you can about why you rated as you did. Please be as explicit as possible. You may consult your notes to help you formulate your comments.

(3) After you have completed your rating and made your comments on the first speaker's performance, rate the remaining three speakers following the same procedure. Note that because the test tapes were assembled in a random fashion, it is possible, although quite unlikely, that all four speakers will be of equal ability.

(4) When you have completed your ratings for all four speakers, you will be given four short questionnaires--one to be filled out for each speaker. At this time you may replay any segment of the test tape again if you wish.

NOTE: DO NOT RESERVE THE '1' AND '5' RATINGS FOR READINGS WHICH ARE 'ABSOLUTELY INCOMPREHENSIBLE' OR 'COMPLETELY NATIVE-LIKE'.

SUBJECT RATING SHEET

Rating Scale:	5 – high
	4
	3 – mid
	2
	1 – low

Rater Code:_____

Tape No._____

Rating_____   How many times did you listen to this
                    tape segment?_____

Comments:

RATING QUESTIONNAIRE 'A'

Rater Code:_____

Tape No. _____

(1) From what area of the world do you think this subject comes?
_____ Africa (sub-Sahara)
_____ Latin America
_____ Middle East/North Africa
_____ Southeast Asia
_____ Europe

(2) What do you think the subject's native language is?

_____

(3) On the following scale, please indicate with an 'X' how well
the subject seemed to understand what he was reading.

Not at all   Completely

1   2   3   4   5   6   7   8   9

DIRECTIONS FOR RATING TAPE SEGMENTS 'B'

Task	In this part of the experiment, you will rate how well some non-native speakers communicate in English. They will be retelling, in their own words, the prose passage they read as their first task. At this time, please rate the speakers on how well they 'communicate'--not on how well they 'remember' the prose passage.

Rating Training Tapes	First, listen to all four speakers on the Training Tape. Then replay the tape and rate the speakers' performances using the 5-point scale shown on the 'Subject Rating Sheet'.

Rating Test Tapes

(1) After you have rated the speakers on the training tape, listen to the first speaker on the Test Tape. DO NOT STOP THE TAPE UNTIL HE HAS FINISH-ED SPEAKING. You may then replay the tape segment as many times as you wish before you decide on your rating. It is important, however, that you indicate on the 'Subject Rating Sheet' the number of times you replayed this segment. As you listen, you may want to take notes about the speaker's performance to help you decide on your rating. For these notes, use the separate note paper provided for this purpose.

(2) When you have decided on the rating, put it on the 'Subject Rating Sheet' and then make any comments you can about why you rated as you did. Please be as explicit as possible. You may consult your notes to help you formulate your comments.

(3) After you have completed your rating and made your comments on the first speaker's performance, rate the remaining three speakers following the same procedure. Note that because the test tapes were assembled in a random fashion, it is possible, although quite unlikely, that all four speakers will be of equal ability.

(4) When you have completed your ratings for all four speakers, you will be given four short questionnaires--one to be filled out for each speaker. At this time you may replay any segment of the test tape again if you wish.

NOTE: DO NOT RESERVE THE '1' AND '5' RATINGS FOR READINGS WHICH ARE 'ABSOLUTELY INCOMPREHENSIBLE' OR 'COMPLETELY NATIVE-LIKE'.

RATING QUESTIONNAIRE 'B'

Rater Code:_____
Tape No.:_____

(1) The subject's retelling of the written passage was:
_____ excellent
_____ good
_____ fair
_____ poor

(2) Please check the appropriate line for each of the following pairs of adjectives to indicate the impressions you got about the subject's mood and personality.

1.	_____ eager	:	_____ hesitant
2.	_____ tense	:	_____ relaxed
3.	_____ worried	:	_____ confident
4.	_____ pleasant	:	_____ disagreeable
5.	_____ boring	:	_____ interesting
6.	_____ cooperative	:	_____ antagonistic
7.	_____ optimistic	:	_____ pessimistic
8.	_____ dull	:	_____ bright

DIRECTIONS FOR RATING TAPE SEGMENTS 'D'

Purpose of Experiment: To develop a better and more reliable method of assessing spoken language proficiency of non-native speakers of English.

Task   In this part of the experiment, you will rate how well some non-native speakers communicate in English. Each speaker will tell about a holiday or festival which is celebrated in his country.

Rating   First, listen to all four speakers on the Training
Training   Tape. Then replay the training tape and, using the
Tapes   5-point scale shown on the 'Rating Sheet', rate how well each speaker was able to communicate in English. Note that these speakers were chosen to demonstrate a wide range in speaking ability. When you listen to the test tape, it is unlikely that you will hear any speaker who is much better or much worse than the best or poorest speakers on the training tape. Therefore, do not reserve the '1' and '5' ratings for speech

which is 'absolutely incomprehensible' or 'completely native-like'.

Rating Test Tapes

(1) After you have rated the speakers on the training tape, listen to the first speaker on the Test Tape. DO NOT STOP THE TAPE until he has finished speaking. You may then replay the tape segment as many times as you wish before you decide on your rating. It is important, however, that you indicate on the 'Subject Rating Sheet' the number of times you replayed this segment. As you listen, you may want to take notes about the speaker's performance to help you decide on your rating. For these notes, use the separate note paper provided for this purpose.

(2) When you have decided on the rating, put it on the 'Subject Rating Sheet' and then make any comments you can about why you rated as you did. Please be as explicit as possible. You may consult your notes to help you formulate your comments.

(3) After you have completed your rating and made your comments on the first speaker's performance, rate the remaining three speakers following the same procedure. Note that because the test tapes were assembled in a random fashion, it is possible, although quite unlikely, that all four speakers will be of equal ability.

(4) When you have completed your ratings for all four speakers, you will be given four short questionnaires--one to be filled out for each speaker. At this time you may replay any segment of the test tape again if you wish.

RATING QUESTIONNAIRE 'D'

Rater Code:_____
Tape No.:_____

(1) On the following scale, indicate with an 'X' where you would rate this subject's performance.

Non-English   English

| 1 | 2 | 3 | 4 | 5 | 6 | 7 | 8 | 9 |

(2) Please check your reactions to the following questions:

Yes   No

___   ___   A. Were you disturbed by the way the subject pronounced English?

___   ___   B. Were you bothered by the speed (fast or slow) with which the subject spoke?

___   ___   C. Were you interested in the subject's topic?

___   ___   D. Were you annoyed by some of the things the subject said?
             Explain:_____
             _____

___   ___   E. Were you especially pleased by some of the things the subject said? Explain_____
             _____

___   ___   F. Did you find the subject's voice pleasing?

(3) The following are presumed to be important factors in speech communication. Please indicate those which positively or negatively affected your rating of the subject's performance.

Favorably   Unfavorably

_____   general intelligibility   _____
_____   grammaticality   _____
_____   pronunciation (consonants & vowels)   _____
_____   intonation (stress & pitch)   _____
_____   fluency (general speed)   _____
_____   vocabulary (choice/appropriateness)   _____
_____   content (subject matter)   _____

(4) Please check the appropriate box for each of the following pairs of adjectives to indicate the impressions you got about the subject's mood and personality.

1. _____ eager   : _____ hesitant
2. _____ tense   : _____ relaxed
3. _____ worried   : _____ confident
4. _____ pleasant   : _____ disagreeable
5. _____ boring   : _____ interesting
6. _____ cooperative : _____ antagonistic
7. _____ optimistic   : _____ pessimistic
8. _____ dull   : _____ bright

SUBJECTIVE REACTIONS TOWARD ACCENTED SPEECH[1]

ELLEN BOUCHARD RYAN

University of Notre Dame

As the largest bilingual minority group in the United States, Americans of Mexican origin have been the focus of growing public attention. Of particular concern is the recognition that attitudes toward bilingualism have had a great impact on the levels of social and educational achievement which members of this group attain. In addition to the difficulties of becoming educated through English, often the second language, and of confronting a widespread downgrading of Spanish, Mexican Americans in the Southwest often suffer alienation and discrimination because of their accented speech.

According to Ortego (1970), the vast majority of bilingual, and monolingual, Mexican Americans in the Southwest speak English with an unmistakable influence from Spanish phonology. Even if a Mexican American is monolingual, he is likely to have an accent if most of the English he hears is spoken by Mexican Americans, with varying degrees of accentedness. Actually, several authors (Metcalf 1970, Ortego 1970) have proposed that Mexican American speech be considered as a dialect of English in a manner similar to black dialect.

Ortego (1970) states further that an accent can reduce chances for educational and occupational success if it serves to evoke a prejudicial attitude in the listener toward the speaker. In an early study, Barker (1947) noted that many Mexican American bilinguals manifested a feeling of inferiority with respect to the 'Mexican accent' in their spoken English. The association of inferior social status with this accent was so strong that some parents spoke only English to their children in the hope that they would grow up without an accent and thus have broader opportunities.

Evaluative reactions toward speakers of various languages or dialects have been widely studied during the last fifteen years. Since Wallace Lambert and his colleagues originally developed the matched-guise technique for comparing reactions to two languages, adapted forms have been employed to assess biases toward different varieties of the same language: Canadian French and European French (Preston 1963). Standard English and Jewish-accented English (Anisfeld, Bogo, and Lambert 1962); Standard English and French-Canadian accented English (Webster and Kramer 1968); and varieties of White and Black English for several social classes (Tucker and Lambert 1969, Shuy 1969, Bouchard-Ryan 1969).

In the only published study involving attitudes toward Mexican-American English, Williams, Whitehead, and Miller (1971) analyzed teacher evaluations of children's speech. Anglo and black teachers rated Mexican-American children reliably more 'ethnic-nonstandard' than anglo children whereas Mexican-American teachers did not display different reactions toward the two groups. Clearly, the speech of the Mexican-American children served as a social marker for the anglo and the black judges. According to Williams (1970), reactions to speech might be linked to attitudes and other behaviors in the following manner:

in a situation, (1) speech types serve as social identifiers. (2) These elicit stereotypes held by ourselves and others (including ones of ourselves). (3) We tend to behave in accord with these stereotypes, and thus (4) translate our attitudes into a social reality.

More information about evaluative reactions could be obtained in further investigations if the differences between speech styles were quantified. None of the previous studies have specified the linguistic characteristics on the basis of which group's speech style differs from another. Although the usual method of selecting speakers is based on sociological criteria such as ethnic group and socioeconomic class, it is clear that there is great variation in accentedness among Mexican Americans within any such sociological categories (Grebler, Moore, and Guzman 1970). It would seem necessary, then, to develop procedures for measuring the degree of accentedness before conducting any program of research concerning the subjective reactions of various groups toward accented speech.

The purpose of this study is to introduce an approach toward the quantification of accentedness and to suggest experiments concerning evaluative reactions of Mexican-American bilinguals and anglos for which accentedness scores will be needed.

Development of accentedness measures

The term accentedness has been defined for bilinguals as 'the degree to which the phonological and syntactic structures of one language appear to influence speech produced in the other' (Terry and Cooper 1971). For the purpose of this discussion, however, accentedness will be operationally defined in terms of the degree to which only the phonological structures of Spanish influence speech produced in English by bilingual Mexican Americans. The speech samples will consist of taped readings of prepared passages in order to control for the variations in syntax and vocabulary that would appear in spontaneous speech. Once we have obtained a clear notion of the phonological aspects characteristic of accentedness, we can extend our study to include the analysis of spontaneous speech where accentedness will certainly be more evident than in text reading.

Two major goals have motivated the search for reliable measures of accentedness. On a theoretical level, we need a description of the major pronunciation differences contributing to apparent accentedness in the English speech of Mexican Americans. On a more practical level, the assignment of accentedness scores which are consistent with intuitive reactions to speech is necessary in order to study the role of accentedness in interpersonal behavior, especially language attitudes.

Suggested procedures. Labov (1966, 1970) has been a leader among sociolinguists in his design of methodology for the description of speech styles of members of various social strata. He has established the notion of the phonological variable, which has allowed the sociolinguist to characterize various speech styles according to the relative frequency with which certain specific pronunciations occur (Shuy 1969, Ma and Herasimchuk 1971). For example, the substitution of the stop /t/ for the fricative /θ/ in words such as 'thing' and 'three' by speakers in New York City becomes systematically more frequent the lower the social class and the more informal the speaking situation (Labov 1966).

The application of the techniques developed by Labov lead to a promising approach to the study of Spanish accentedness in English speech. Initially, a number of phonological variables are selected according to criteria which include frequency of substitutions in accented speech as well as the reliability of their detection by linguistically-trained judges. The phonological variables to be considered in our original analysis have been selected on the basis of the contrastive analysis of English and Spanish by Stockwell and Bowen (1965) and pilot work with the reading samples of thirty-five bilingual speakers. See the Appendix for the list of suprasegmentals, vowels, and consonants which are applied in our analysis. Additional variables suggested by Ornstein (1971) in his discussion of Mexican-American speech are also mentioned in the Appendix.

Once the phonological indices have been chosen, the standard reading passages must be prepared. The passages are written in informal English in order to elicit maximum accentedness in the readings (see Labov 1966, and Ma and Herasimchuk 1971). Contained in the readings are ten specific opportunities for each of the ten specified phonological substitutions typical of highly accented speech to occur. In this manner, each variable is given equal weight despite the fact that the overall frequency in natural speech of some variables is much higher than that of others. Furthermore, ten options to pronounce a phoneme with accent should provide an adequate sample of individual performance without undue textual length. To allow for tests of reliability in phonological measures across two texts, it would be best to prepare two sets of comparable readings.

The next step in the procedure involves the selection of a sample of bilingual Mexican Americans with a wide range of accentedness in their English speech. After hearing instructions intended to make the situation as informal as possible, each subject reads the texts; and his performance is recorded on magnetic tape. From the tapes, three trained listeners independently rate the pronunciations of each variable in each of the ten specified locations, and the inter-judge reliability of the ratings is determined. On the basis of these ratings, a relative frequency score for each of the variables, based on the proportion of the pronunciations which are accented, is obtained for each subject. See Table 1 for a schema of results thus far.

TABLE 1. Relative frequency scores for phonological variables.

Subjects	Variables V_1	V_2	V_3	$V_4 \cdots$	V_{10}
1	$p_{1,1}$	$p_{1,2}$	$p_{1,3}$	$p_{1,4} \cdots$	$p_{1,10}$
.					.
.					.
.					.
n	$p_{n,1}$	$p_{n,2}$	$p_{n,3}$	$p_{n,4} \cdots$	$p_{n,10}$

A major question still remains unanswered: how the collection of relative frequency scores for each subject should be combined into a

single accentedness score. At this point, a consideration of psychophysical scaling procedures would seem fruitful.

Psychophysical scaling techniques (Stevens and Galancer 1957) were
originally devised in order to determine the relationship between
changes in a physical dimension and the corresponding changes in
human perception--for example, apparent loudness as a function of
the intensity of a sound signal or apparent brightness as a function of
the intensity of a light signal. In addition, however, similar techniques have been developed for placing various stimuli on a ratio
scale even when there is no evidence for a single underlying physical
dimension. Direct scaling methods have been employed to scale such
phenomena as attitudes and opinions (Stevens 1968), esthetic value of
handwriting samples (Ekman and Kunnepas 1960), prestige of occupations (Perloe 1963), and pronunciability of trigrams (Dawson and
Brinker 1970).

Probably the only similar technique utilized by sociolinguists has
been the category scale, which has been employed frequently to measure subjective reactions to speech styles. Indeed, several attempts
have been made to produce category scales of accentedness. In
Fishman, Cooper, and Ma (1971), Puerto Rican bilingual speakers
were rated by trained judges using a 7-point scale with high scores
indicating much Spanish influence on English speech and low scores
indicating much English influence on Spanish speech. One of the
difficulties with this scale lies in the fact that a neutral score is presumably assigned both to a person with native-like speech in both his
languages and to a person with much interference in both his languages.
Grebler, Moore, and Guzman (1970) asked survey takers, without
special linguistic training to rate both the Spanish and English speech
of Mexican-American respondents by means of a 3-point category
scale: very fluent, normally fluent, and broken English/Spanish. In
both of these studies, however, the category scales were merely part
of a large number of measures; and little attempt was made to test
their reliability.

The development of a more sophisticated approach to accentedness
scaling which would provide a direct measure of the naive (non-lin-
guistically trained) listener's judgment of accentedness is a crucial
prerequisite for any systematic investigation of sociolinguistic aspects
of accentedness. In our laboratory Muench (1971) has conducted a
pilot study on the psychophysical scaling of accentedness. Excerpts
of eight speakers reading the same English passage were selected
from the readings of thirty-five Spanish-English bilingual speakers
in such a way that a wide range of accentedness was represented.
These speech samples were presented to twenty-four Notre Dame
undergraduates who were asked to judge how accented the speech of
each sample appeared to them by estimating the degree to which each

sample appeared to them by estimating the degree to which each sample was unlike standard English speech. Their opinions were elicited in two consecutive tasks by magnitude estimation and by sensory modality matching. In the magnitude estimation task, each subject was asked to assign a number to the first speaker estimating the degree of accentedness which he perceived in that speech sample. Subsequent speakers were to be assigned numbers estimating accentedness in proportion to the first judgment. In the sensory modality matching task, the subject heard the same samples a second time in another order and was asked to squeeze a hand dynamometer with a force proportional to the degree of perceived accentedness.

An accentedness scale was then obtained by calculating the median magnitude estimation for each speaker as judged by the twenty-four raters. Similarly a median sensory modality matching scale was established. The rankings in both scales are in perfect agreement, with Spearman Rho = 1.00. The ranking agreement shows a consistency in the two measures with respect to the entire group of judges. This result suggests that at least an ordinal scale of accentedness can be developed, and it is expected that data of an interval or ratio nature might be obtained in later experiments. In further work, the degree of agreement among individual raters will be determined by an analysis using Kendall's Coefficient of Concordance (W).

Subsequent experiments should include groups to counterbalance order of tasks, and the reliability of the scaling should be found by sampling different raters from the same population. Also, in order to obtain a reliable accentedness score for a single speaker, different reading samples by the same subject should be compared. Eventually, this method should produce an accentedness score for an individual using a minimal speech sample. For purposes of the following discussion, an interval scale will be assumed.

After we have obtained an accentedness score for each subject, we can add this information to our phonological-variable matrix, as in Table 2. A series of paired correlations will be computed to determine which phonological variables vary together thus providing overlapping, redundant information, and which are most in agreement with the psychophysical scalings of accentedness. Multiple regression analysis (Morrison 1967) can be used to select the best equation for predicting the psychophysical scores on the basis of a small number of the phonological variables. Thus it is through the psychophysical scaling procedures that the weightings of the phonological variables can be determined. Once the equation is known, a method is available for assigning an accentedness score to a speech sample on the basis of a fairly brief phonological analysis. Therefore, the time-consuming tasks involved in psychophysical scaling need only be utilized temporarily, until a valid and reliable method based on

relative frequency scores of a few phonological variables is
developed.

TABLE 2. Relative frequency scores for phonological variables
and accentedness scores.

Subjects	Accentedness scores	Phonological variables			
		V_1	V_2	$V_3...$	V_{10}
1	a_1	$p_{1,1}$	$p_{1,2}$	$p_{1,3}$	$p_{1,10}$
2					
.					
.					
.					
n	a_n	$p_{n,1}$	$p_{n,2}$	$p_{n,3}$	$p_{n,10}$

Several research questions based on use of accentedness measures.
Three variables affecting the degree of apparent accentedness should
be considered: (1) relationship to speaker's proficiency and usage of
English, (2) effect of sociolinguistic context, and (3) effect of listener
characteristics.

To what extent can the degree of accentedness be predicted from a
speaker's knowledge of English vocabulary, grammar, and idioms
and from the relative frequency of his use of English as compared to
Spanish? It is clear that a person with little knowledge of English
who uses English infrequently will speak with a strong accent. However, if all the English one hears is heavily accented, one might have
an accent quite unrelated to proficiency and use of English. Furthermore, it seems that two persons with equivalent language experience
and proficiency may have quite different degrees of accentedness due
to individual differences in personality. The relationships among
accentedness, language knowledge, and language use can be determined through correlational methods applied to scores for accentedness and for tests of proficiency and use obtained from a sample of
subjects. If the associations with these other variables are weak,
then it is indeed important to study accentedness as a separate factor.

Another important question concerns the variation in accentedness
observed for the same speaker in different speech situations. Labov
(1966) and Ma and Herasimchuk (1971) have noted systematic increases
in nonstandard pronunciations as the style context becomes more informal, from list and text reading through careful and casual speech.

It is most likely that the features of accented pronunciations among bilingual Mexican Americans are also subject to such stylistic variations. This prediction can be tested by asking each of a group of subjects to perform a series of tasks, including reading and spontaneous speech, which are intended to elicit a wide range of speech styles. The same accentedness equation obtained for reading can probably be applied to spontaneous speech without, however, controlled overall frequencies for the opportunities of the critical phonological variables. It would also be interesting to determine whether the ranking of subjects according to accentedness is similar for all speech styles. Greater accentedness would be expected in English spoken among Mexican Americans than in English spoken to Anglos. Even among Mexican Americans, less accentedness may be expected in Anglo-oriented places such as school, work, or government than in Mexican-American-oriented places such as home or neighborhood.

By shifting the spotlight from the speaker to the listener, one can investigate the differences among the psychophysical scales of accentedness based on the subjective reactions to accentedness of monolingual Anglo speakers of standard English who have had no contact with Mexican Americans, of monolingual Anglo speakers of standard English who have had frequent contact with Mexican Americans, and of bilingual Mexican Americans. It is expected that experience with accented speech probably leads to greater sensitivity toward the non-standard pronunciations. It is more difficult to predict whether or not, for Mexican Americans, the sensitivity of accented speakers is less than that of unaccented speakers.

Accentedness and language attitudes

With a reliable method for assigning an accentedness score to a speaker, it is possible to test a number of predictions concerning the relation between accentedness of bilingual Mexican Americans and language attitudes.

For bilingual Mexican Americans, it is relevant to study not only reactions to native-like English and native-like Spanish but also toward various degrees of accentedness in English speech. This is the case because both Spanish and Spanish-accented English can serve to identify a speaker as Mexican American. In such an experiment, taped speech samples representing four levels of accentedness can be presented to groups of Mexican American and Anglo listeners for ratings on semantic differential scales. One level, including no accentedness, would be standard English.

This experiment can provide data concerning the degree to which listeners distinguish among the four levels of accentedness. In the discussion section following the paper of Shuy (1969), David DeCamp mentioned that he and his associates at the University of Texas had been using the semantic differential to study listener's reactions to speech styles. His student, Scott Baird, had just completed a dissertation in which reactions were elicited for speech samples representing a continuum of styles ranging from inclusion of a maximum number of black dialect features to a total lack of such features. Among the 92-93% of the raters who recognized the speakers as Negro, the prejudicial reactions overrode all other responses. Thus, although the nonstandard features included in the speech samples gradually increased, a minimum amount of nonstandardness was sufficient to elicit the complete stereotype of a black. It appears that language merely served to identify the speaker's group membership. This type of categorical, rather than gradually changing, reaction may also be prevalent in our study with standard English and three levels of accented speech. It will be most interesting to determine whether all accented speech elicits the same reaction or whether a gradual shift occurs as the accentedness becomes stronger. It is possible that the reaction of the Mexican Americans would be more gradual than that of the Anglos because of greater experience with people of varying accents.

In order to assess the differences between reactions of the two groups of listeners, the dimensions of status and solidarity must be introduced. In his discussion of forms of address, Brown (1965) demonstrated the roles played by status (relative degree to which a person possesses the characteristics valued by the society as a whole) and solidarity (degree to which a person is similar to the perceiver, in terms of group membership, shared experiences, age, socioeconomic class, etc.). Pilot work is currently being conducted by the author which will lead to the incorporation of these dimensions into the semantic differential instrument by the selection of ten scales reflecting solidarity values.

It is hypothesized that both Anglos and Mexican Americans will rate the more strongly accented speech lower on status scales, thus reflecting actual relationships within the whole society. On the other hand, whereas the Anglo will also downgrade the accented speech on the solidarity dimension, the Mexican Americans will rate accented speech on the solidarity dimension, the Mexican Americans will rate accented speech (similar to his own and that of his family and friends) more highly on the solidarity dimension, reflecting a greater affinity for and identification with the speaker. Thus, greater similarity in status ratings, which reflect a society-wide situation, among different groups of judges is to be expected than in the solidarity ratings, which depend on the rater's identification with the particular speech variety.

Another application of psychophysical methods can allow us to further examine the differences between status and solidarity ratings of accented speech. In a proposed experiment, three groups of bilingual Mexican-American subjects are asked to rate the same eight speech samples using magnitude estimation. The first group provides estimates based on degree of perceived accentedness. The second group provides a measure of socioeconomic status by estimating the level of annual income of the speaker's family. A measure of solidarity is obtained by asking a third group to judge the likelihood of the speaker becoming a personal friend. Paired correlations of the accentedness scalings of the samples with the status and solidarity scalings are computed. If our predictions are correct, high status ratings will be strongly correlated with low accentedness ratings but high solidarity ratings will be correlated with high accentedness ratings.

The reactions of bilingual Mexican Americans to varying degrees of accented speech will certainly not be homogeneous. In addition to socioeconomic class, degree of assimilation, and age, one factor which may be related to the speech attitudes is accentedness of the listener's own speech. Specifically, one would expect the solidarity ratings of strongly accented speech to be higher the more accented the speech of the listener.

The semantic differential ratings assigned to speech samples also depend on the sociolinguistic context. Accentedness or any form of nonstandard speech occurs more frequently in informal situations and is thus likely to be downgraded in such contexts. Furthermore, one would expect raters to be less critical of accented speech in home and neighborhood situations than in school and work situations. Agheyisi and Fishman (1970) have pointed out that judges in the experimental matched-guise setting may be reacting to 'the congruity, or lack of it, between the topic, speaker, and the particular language variety.' By systematically varying the formality of the speech situation as well as the content in terms of characters, locality, and topic, it should be possible to describe the effects of these contextual variables on reactions to speech styles.

Conclusion

This paper has attempted to specify ways in which accentedness, as an important sociolinguistic variable, can be fruitfully investigated. A methodological approach, which combines sociolinguistic and psychophysical techniques, has been proposed for the measurement of accentedness in the English speech of bilingual Mexican Americans. With accentedness as a dependent variable, relationships between the degree of perceived accentedness and characteristics of the speaker, listener, and sociolinguistic context can be studied. As an independent variable, degree of accentedness can be utilized to categorize speech styles in experiments investigating evaluative reactions toward speech of groups of listeners of varying ethnic group, socioeconomic class, age, and accentedness of their own speech.

The study of accentedness can be expanded in many directions. As already mentioned, a natural extention of the analysis of their Spanish-accented English among bilingual Mexican Americans would be the analysis of their English-accented Spanish. Furthermore, the proposed approach could easily be applied to any group with several speech varieties differing in pronunciation, such as blacks, Puerto Ricans, and the French Americans of New England and Louisiana. Also, the wide range of psychophysical techniques could be explored in the hope of finding additional procedures which could be of use in the scaling of reactions toward accented speech.

NOTE

[1] The author would like to acknowledge her gratitude to Eileen Muench and Sharon Ohlweiler for their valuable contributions in the formulation of the ideas presented here.

REFERENCES

Agheyisi, R. and J. A. Fishman. 1970. Language attitude studies: a brief survey of methodological approaches. Anthropological Linguistics. 12(5).137-57.
Anisfeld, M., N. Bogo, and W. E. Lambert. 1962. Evaluational reactions to accented English speech. Journal of Abnormal and Social Psychology. 63.223-31.
Barker, G. C. 1947. Social functions of language in a Mexican-American community. Acta Americana. 5.185-202.
Bouchard-Ryan, E. 1969. A psycholinguistic attitude study. Studies in Language and Language Behavior. 8.437-50.
Brown, R. 1965. Social psychology. New York, Free Press.
Dawson, W. E. and R. P. Brinker. 1971. Validation of ratio scales of opinion by multimodality matching. Perception and Psychophysics. 9(5).413-17.
Ekman, G. and T. Kunnepas. 1960. Note on direct and indirect scaling methods. Psychological Reports. 17.174.
Fishman, J. A., R. L. Cooper, and R. Ma. eds. 1971. Bilingualism in the barrio. Language Science Monographs, No. 7. Bloomington Ind., Research Center in Anthropology, Folklore, and Linguistics.
Grebler, L., J. W. Moore, and R. C. Guzman, eds. 1970. The Mexican American people. New York, The Free Press.

Labov, W. 1966. The social stratification of English in New York City. Washington, D. C., Center for Applied Linguistics.

Ma, R. and E. Herasimchuk. 1971. Linguistic domains of a bilingual neighborhood. In: Bilingualism in the barrio. Ed. by J. Fishman, R. Cooper, and R. Ma. Bloomington, Ind., Research Center in Anthropology, Folklore, and Linguistics. 349-464.

Metcalf, A. A. 1970. Characteristics of Mexican-American English. Paper presented at the Philological Association of the Pacific Coast, Spokane, Washington.

Morrison, D. F. 1967. Multivariate statistical methods. New York, McGraw-Hill.

Muench, E. 1971. Preliminary report: scaling of accentedness by magnitude estimation. Unpublished manuscript, University of Notre Dame.

Ornstein, J. 1971. Sociolinguistic research on language diversity in the American Southwest and its educational implications. Modern Language Journal. 55(4).223-29.

Ortego, P. D. 1969-70. Some cultural implications of a Mexican American border dialect of American English. Studies in Linguistics. 21.77-84.

Perloe, S. S. 1963. The relation between category-rating and magnitude-estimation judgments of occupational prestige. American Journal of Psychology. 76.395-403.

Preston, M. S. 1963. Evaluational reactions to English, Canadian French, and European French voices. Unpublished M. A. thesis, McGill University, Redpath Library.

Shuy, R. W. 1969. Subjective judgments in sociolinguistic analysis. In: Linguistics and the teaching of standard English to speakers of other languages or dialects. Ed. by J. E. Alatis. 20th Annual Roundtable, No. 22. Washington, D. C., Georgetown University Press. 175-88.

Stevens, S. S. 1968. Ratio scales of opinion. In: Handbook of measurement and assessment in behavioral sciences. Ed. by D. K. Whitla. Reading, Mass., Addison-Wesley.

_____ and E. Galanter. 1957. Ratio scales and category scales for a dozen perceptual continua. Journal of Experimental Psychology. 54.377-411.

Stockwell, R. P. and J. D. Bowen. 1965. The sounds of English and Spanish. Chicago, University of Chicago Press.

Terry, C. and R. L. Cooper. 1971. The perception of phonological variation. In: Bilingualism in the barrio. Ed. by J. A. Fishman, R. L. Cooper, and R. Ma. Bloomington, Ind., Research Center in Anthropology, Folklore, and Linguistics. 333-36.

Tucker, G. R. and W. E. Lambert. 1969. White and Negro listeners' reactions to various American-English dialects. Social Forces. 47.463-68.

Webster, W. G. and E. Kramer. 1968. Attitudes and evaluational
reactions to accented English speech. Journal of Social Psychology.
75.231-40.
Williams, F. 1970. Language, attitudes, and social change. In:
Language and poverty. Ed. by F. Williams. Chicago, Markham
Publishing Co.
_____, J. R. Whitehead, and L. M. Miller. 1971. Attitudinal
correlates of children's speech characteristics. USOE Report.
Austin, Center for Communications Research, University of Texas.

APPENDIX

Phonological variables for accentedness study

Suprasegmentals

(1) Omission of middle accent (ˋ) in polysyllabic words, as in
e ràd i ća tion', 'chàr ac ter ís tic', and 'tèr min á tion'.
(2) Regular syllable length (in terms of time) as opposed to the
usual English extension of time for stressed syllables and reduced
time for unstressed syllables, as in 'to mor row', 'hap pen ing', and
're al iz a tion'.

Stressed Vowels

(3) Substitution of [a] for [æ] in words as 'bat' and 'happen'.
(4) Substitution of [i] for [I] in words as 'bit' and 'lift'.
(5) Substitution of rounded [o] for [ow] in words such as 'boat'
and 'slow'.
(6) Substitution of [u] for [U] in words such as 'good' and 'could'.

Consonants

(7) Substitution of voiceless [s] for voiced [z] in words such as
'appeased' and 'residence'.
(8) Substitution of voiced [z] for voiceless [s] before juncture or
pause, as in 'yes ter day' and 'dis cov er'.
(9) Substitution of epenthetic [e] before initial [s] followed by
consonant as in 'Spanish' and 'scream'.
(10) Substitution of [b] or [f] for [v] as in 'rave' and 'vain'.

Other phonological variables, suggested by Ornstein (1971)

(a) /č/ and /š/ alteration

(b) Realization of /θ/ – /ð/ and /t/ – /d/
(c) Substitution of [ʃ] for y

ANATOMICAL AND CULTURAL DETERMINANTS OF MALE AND FEMALE SPEECH

JACQUELINE SACHS, PHILIP LIEBERMAN, AND
DONNA ERICKSON

University of Connecticut

It is usually possible to differentiate the speech of normal, adult male and female speakers of English. It is not clear whether the factors that enable listeners to categorize a voice as either female or male are wholly dependent on anatomical differences between the male and female speech producing equipment, or whether learned, culturally prescribed factors also play a part in defining the norms for male and female voice quality.

Culturally determined differences in men's and women's speech certainly exist in some languages. For example, Haas (1964) has reported sex-determined styles in the American Indian language of Koasati. In Thai, according to Haas, the differences are quite evident since the language requires different sets of lexical items for men and women. In English we also see some stylistic differences in vocabulary though they are not very large. The focus of this study is, however, not on these rather evident lexical aspects of sexual differentiation but on basic phonetic factors.

When adult male and female voices are phonetically differentiated the most obvious factor is pitch, or fundamental frequency of phonation. The lower fundamental frequencies of the male are a consequence of secondary sexual dimorphism that occurs at puberty (Negus 1949, Kirchner 1970). The larynx of the male is enlarged and the vocal cords become longer and thicker. Although pitch is the most obvious perceptual factor recent studies have demonstrated that it is

possible to differentiate adult male and female speakers of English
with no information about fundamental frequency (e. g. Schwartz 1968,
Schwartz and Rine 1968). In all likelihood, the relevant cue for these
discriminations is the pattern of formant frequencies, or resonances
of the supralaryngeal vocal tract. It is quite reasonable that the sex
of the speaker should be identifiable from the formants. Secondary
sexual dimorphism causes males, on the average, to have larger
supralaryngeal vocal tracts than females, leading to a pattern of lower
formant frequencies. In Figure 1 we have reproduced the data obtained by Peterson and Barney (1952) for the vowel formants of a
sample of seventy-six adult males, adult females, and children who
were all speakers of General American English. Each phonetic
symbol represents a token of a vowel for an individual speaker. The
frequency of the second formant is plotted with respect to the vertical
axis while the first formant is plotted with respect to the horizontal
axis. Note that there is no single data point for a particular vowel;
there are instead regions defined by these loops.

There are, however, some rather puzzling aspects to the actual
acoustic disparities that exist between adult male and female speakers.
Mattingly (1966) in a reanalysis of the Peterson and Barney data,
showed that the acoustic differences are greater than one would expect
if the sole determining factor were simply the average anatomical
difference that exists between adult men and women. It is possible
that adult men and women modify their articulation of the same phonetic elements to produce acoustic signals that correspond to the
male-female archetypes. In other words, men tend to talk as though
they were bigger, and women as though they were smaller, than they
actually may be. Since these effects of acculturation would have to be
acquired in childhood it becomes reasonable to test Mattingly's hypothesis by examining the speech production of children, to see
whether they, in fact, acquire male-female speech distinctions.

Anatomical studies have demonstrated that the larynx of a pre-
adolescent boy or girl is likely to be the same size given the same
weight and height (Kirchner 1970). Therefore, one would expect pre-
adolescent children to have essentially the same fundamental frequencies regardless of sex. There is no difference in mandible
length between boys and girls before puberty (Walker and Kowalski
1971, Hunter and Garn 1971). Since mandible length accounts for
half of the supralaryngeal tract length, we can reasonably assume
that prepubertal boys and girls of the same height and weight have the
same supralaryngeal vocal tract size. Therefore, one would not expect the formant frequencies of boys and girls to differ. If they do
differ, the difference may reflect acculturation to the male and female
sex roles. Our present study had two purposes. First, to see whether

FIGURE 1.   Formant frequencies of American-English vowels
for a sample of seventy-six adult men, adult women,
and children (Peterson and Barney 1952).

Note: Closed loops inclose 90% of the data points in each vowel
category.

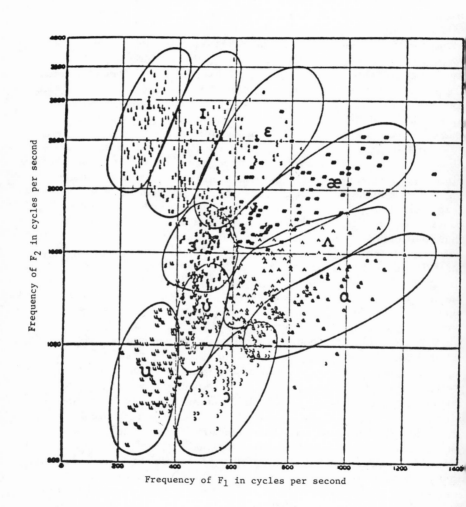

Frequency of F₁ in cycles per second

boys and girls have acquired voice characteristics before puberty that allow their voices to be identified as to sex, and second, to see whether differences in formant frequencies play a role in this differentiation.

Methods

Short samples of speech were recorded for twenty-six children who ranged in age from 4 to 14 years. There were fourteen boys and twelve girls in this group. Each child repeated a short sentence I thought I saw a big blue meanie outside, read a passage from a children's book and repeated the sustained vowels /a/, /i/, and /u/. The children were all recorded at home using a Sony TC800 recorder and Sony microphone which had a flat frequency response to 8 kHz. The children were all from middle-class backgrounds and had all lived in the Storrs, Connecticut area for at least four years, with the exception of one child who had recently arrived from Kansas and two who had spent a year in England during the previous academic year. All were monolingual except for one child who was from a bilingual Korean-English background. These children exhibited no unusual behavior with regard to our acoustic analysis.

A tape was constructed consisting of the twenty-six imitations of the sentence in a random order. Eighty-three adult judges listened to this tape and attempted to identify each voice as a boy or a girl.

A sound spectrograph was used to make normal wide and narrow bandwidth spectrograms and quantized wide bandwidth spectrograms of all sustained vowels. Formant frequencies and fundamental frequencies were determined from these spectrograms.

Results and discussion

Analysis of the sex identification data indicated that the answer to our first question--can judges distinguish the sex of children from their voices?--was an unqualified yes. The adult judges reliably and validly, identified the sex of the children from their voices ($t = 51.13$, $df = 82$, $p < .001$). Eighty-one percent of the guesses were correct. Twelve of the fourteen boys' voices were identified as boys, and nine of the twelve girls were identified as girls. Two girls were overwhelmingly misidentified as boys.

To answer the second question--are differences in formant characteristics involved in this identification?--we analyzed the frequency measurements of the isolated vowels, /a/, /i/, and /u/. Nine pairs of boys' and girls' voices were formed from our original sample of twenty-six by matching on height and weight. The mean height for the nine boys and girls was fifty-two inches, and the mean weight sixty-two pounds. The average age of the girls was older than the boys by four months. For these pairs, we did not include any child over twelve years. This matching of children in pairs was to insure against voice differences that were merely a reflection of a difference in anatomical structure.

If no sex-difference exists for the vowels, one would predict the same fundamental frequency and the same formant frequencies for the boys and girls. This pattern was not obtained.

Table 1 shows the average fundamental frequency for the boys and the girls on the left. On the right is the average formant frequency values for F_1 and F_2 of /a/, /i/, and /u/. For the nine pairs analyzed, the average fundamental frequency was higher for the boys than for the girls ($t = 2.54$, $df = 8$, $p < .05$). It would be most unlikely that the judges used this cue, higher fundamental for the boys, in accurately identifying the sex of the child.

Taking the obtained formant frequency values for all the vowels together, the boys yield lower values than the girls, though not significantly ($t = 1.92$, $df = 53$, $p < .06$). There are a number of reasons to eliminate the vowel /a/ from our consideration at this point. For example, it is the least identifiable of the vowels (Peterson and Barney 1952) and quite subject to dialect variation. We will return to a discussion of /a/ separately below.

TABLE 1. Mean fundamental and formant frequencies for nine pairs of boys and girls, matched on height and weight.

| | /a/ | | | /i/ | | /u/ | |
	F0	F1	F2	F1	F2	F1	F2
Girls	249	968	1568	321	3247	420	1173
Boys	274	932	1611	302	3136	352	975

The formant values for the vowels /i/ and /u/ were significantly lower for the boys than for the girls ($t = 2.33$, $df = 35$, $p < .05$). This pattern of lower formants for the males is the same pattern we find in adult speakers. The judges' success in identification may have been based, in part, on this difference in the formant patterns between the boys and girls.

In the nine pairs of children we have been discussing there were many children who were well-identified, but also a few who were inconsistently identified, or misidentified as to sex. Let us now look at the characteristics that lead to accurate or poor identification within one sex. From the original twenty-six children, we again formed pairs matched on height to eliminate gross differences in anatomical structure and development. These pairs consisted of three of the best-identified children and three of the worst-identified children, for each sex. Table 2 shows the fundamental and formants for the best and worst boys and girls. For the boys, we find a similar pattern to that which we saw when comparing boys and girls. The most boy-like voices have higher fundamentals but lower formants. The correlation overall between lowness of formants and probability of identifying a boy's voice as a boy is significant (t = .67, df = 13, p < .01).

TABLE 2. Mean fundamental and formant frequencies for the three best and three least identified voices, for each sex, matched on height.

		/a/		/i/		/u/	
	F0	F1	F2	F1	F2	F1	F2
Boys							
Best identified	270	944	1370	315	3278	315	982
Least identified	248	926	1574	352	3352	444	1111
Girls							
Best identified	234	982	1593	333	3370	426	1222
Least identified	260	963	1611	296	2944	426	1148

For the girls, the pattern is the mirror-image. The most girl-like voices have lower fundamentals and higher formants. However, there were some girls with relatively low formants who were still judged accurately, and the correlation between highness of formants and probability of identifying a girl's voice as a girl was not significant (t = .50, df = 10, p < .05). Perhaps some other characteristics indicated that these were feminine voices to the judges. We will return to this topic in a moment.

The girls who were least identifiable as girls include two who were overwhelmingly identified as boys (by 81% and 86% of our sample, respectively). These two girls were not the tallest or heaviest in our sample. They had formant patterns close to the boys' average. A neighbor who knew nothing of the aims of the experiment or the results, was asked to describe these girls. In one case, the girl was sketched as 'athletic, strong, and competitive', and in the other as 'a tomboy, very sports-minded, a real tough kid but well liked'.

Of course, these data are merely suggestive, but we feel further investigation of the relationship between personality and acquisition of like-sex characteristics would be worthwhile.

To summarize the experimental results: Judges could reliably and validly identify the sex of children from their voices. Boys on the average had higher fundamentals but lower formants than girls. The most boy-like voices and the least girl-like voices also showed this same pattern. There are several possibilities we can suggest to explain these results.

First, perhaps past claims about equality in skeletal structure, and thus articulatory structure, are not correct. If the boys, and the girls identified as boys, had larger vocal tracts, the lower formants would result from this anatomical difference. The recent data of Walker and Kowalski (1972) argue against this. Furthermore, the present data suggest disparities between size and formant patterns. First, in the case of the vowel /a/, the boys showed a higher F_2 than did the girls matched on height (with a mean of 1611 for boys and 1568 for girls). Though this difference is not statistically significant, it is different in direction from the difference found for all other formants. This apparent inconsistency in the data may be explainable if we consider the formant pattern for /a/. To make the vowel /a/, both F_1 and F_2 are pulled from the neutral schwa-like position to a more intermediate value, a higher F_1 and F_2. The more /a/ is closer to the ideal, the more F_1 and F_2 converge. However, if some boys are attempting to lower their formants, and especially F_1, they would be able to keep F_1 low by pronouncing /a/ somewhat more centrally, with a lower F_1 and higher F_2. If the boys' articulatory mechanism were simply larger than that of the matched girls, we would expect both F_1 and F_2 to be lower. The data suggest, furthermore, that it is the younger boys who tend to lower the F_1 of /a/. Whereas formants are expected to become lower as height increases, for the boys F_1 of /a/ increases actually, though not significantly, with age ($r = +.15$, $df = 13$). For all other formants measured in this study, the expected negative correlation between value of formant and height was found. These values are shown in Table 3.

Inspection of Table 3 also reveals that the girls' formant values are following their increase in height more closely than the boys' values, with the exception of F_2 of /i/.

If there is no average difference in articulatory mechanism size, the differences we have observed could arise from differential use of the anatomy. The children could be learning culturally determined patterns that are viewed as appropriate for each sex. Within the limit of his anatomy, a speaker could change the formant pattern by pronouncing vowels with phonetic variations, or by changing the configuration of the lips. Rounding the lips will lengthen the vocal tract, and lower the formants. Spreading the lips will shorten the vocal tract, and raise the formants. The characteristic way some women have of talking and smiling at the same time would have just this effect.

TABLE 3. Correlations of height and formant frequencies for fourteen boys and eleven girls.

	/a/		/i/		/u/	
	F1	F2	F1	F2	F1	F2
Boys	+.15	-.27	-.38	-.74**	-.29	+.04
Girls	-.36	-.63*	-.64*	-.25	-.56	-.57
*Significant at $p < .05$						
**Significant at $p < .01$						

We do not want to claim that the formant pattern we have reported completely accounts for the judges' ability to identify the sex of the child speaker. In fact, we would argue that only a part of the accuracy depends on that cue. The judges in our study listened to a sentence, not an isolated vowel, and perhaps other features of voice quality, the intonation pattern, pronunciation, and so on, contributed to accuracy more than did the characteristics of the vowels that we have examined. As mentioned earlier, some girls with rather low formants were not confused with boys. In general it seemed to us, subjectively, that boys had a more forceful, definite rhythm than the girls. These impressions merit more investigation.

In spontaneous speech, in fact, we would certainly expect other characteristics of sentence production to differ. Though research in this area has not been extensive, a few examples will illustrate some phenomena in English that may be involved in the differentiation of male and female speakers.

We can see an obvious difference in vocabulary items--men tend to use swear words, while women use 'nice' euphemistic phrases such as 'goodness gracious', etc. There may well be more subtle vocabulary differences in men's and women's speech in American English. Ruth Brend (1971) has noted different intonation patterns. Certain patterns, such as the 'surprise' pattern (O͟h, tha͟t's aw͟ful!) or the 'cheerful' pattern (Are you com/ing? or Good/bye) are used predominantly, if not solely, by women. It has been claimed that, in general, women seem to have more extremes of high and low intonation than do men.

In addition to intonation differentiation we may also see phonological distinctions in men's and women's speech. Fischer (1958) found that lisping tends to be associated with female speech, and that in certain New England dialects boys tend to use in for the present participle ending, while girls tend to use ing. For example: fishin' as compared with fishing.

Some aspects of the sex-determined speech style can be used by a speaker of the other sex if the situation is appropriate. Haas (1964) found that in Koasati, the speech of women differed in certain respects from that of men, and yet the women would use the male forms when teaching a young boy the language, or a male would use the female forms when reporting dialogue in a story. Within our culture, we can see variations in speech style when adults speak to babies (Drach 1969; Brown, Salerno, and Sachs 1972). Some aspects of this speech style may be an exaggeration of features that distinguish feminine from masculine speech, such as higher perceived pitch and variability in intonation. The situations in which people use this speech style have a feature in common--they are what J. P. Scott (1958) has called care-giving, or 'epimeletic', situations. Courting couples sometimes speak a type of 'baby-talk' and some people use it when talking to pets. The care-giving role in our culture is considere most appropriate for females, but both women and men typically are embarrassed about using baby-talk, or claim they don't use it. The negative attitude toward this speech style is not universal, however. Ferguson (1956) reports that in Arabic, both men and women use a conventionalized baby-talk to babies, although it is considered more appropriate for women.

We know little at this time about listener's evaluation of speakers and messages as influenced by the speaker's voice and speech characteristics. Typically, in our culture, having an 'effeminate' voice is a problem for a man. With the amount of overlap in physical structure that exists between men and women, perhaps some men learn, among other things, to lower their formants in order to sound more masculine. We expect that having a voice perceived as 'low pitched' in not a severe handicap for a woman, although an aggressive, 'mascu line' speech style may be. The absence of this aggressive style, however, may cause listeners to regard the feminine speaker as 'lacking in authority', placing the woman who wants to be both womanly and assertive in a difficult position. It would be interesting, for example, to observe the development of girls, like the two mentioned in this study, whose speech is perceived as masculine. Will these girls retain this speech style, or modify it as the acculturation forces become greater in their teens?

The research described today suggests that the pattern of formants in male and female children may not be determined totally by their anatomical structure, and that these patterns are one of the cues that tell us whether a voice is male or female.

REFERENCES

Brend, Ruth. 1971. Male-female differences in American English intonation. Paper given at 7th International Congress of Phonetic Sciences.

Brown, R., R. Salerno, and J. Sachs. 1972. Characteristics of adult speech as a function of age of listener. Working paper No. 6. Language Acquisition Laboratory, University of Conn.

Drach, K. 1969. The language of the parent: a pilot study. Working paper No. 14. Language-Behavior Research Laboratory, University of California, Berkeley.

Ferguson, C. A. 1964. Baby talk in six languages. In: The ethnography of communication. Ed. by J. Gumperz and D. Hymes. American Anthropologist. 66(6).103-14.

Fischer, J. 1958. Social influences in the choice of a linguistic variant. Word. 14.47-56.

Haas, Mary. 1964. Men's and women's speech in Koasati. In: Language in culture and society. Ed. by D. Hymes. New York, Harper and Row.

Hunter, W. S. and Stanley Garn. 1972. Disproportiate sexual dimorphism in the human face. American Journal Physical Anthropology. 36.133-38.

Kirchner, J. A. 1970. Physiology of the larynx. Revised ed. Rochester, Minn., American Academy Opthal. and Otolaryngology.

Mattingly, I. 1966. Speaker variation and vocal tract size. Journal of Acoustical Society of America. Abstract.

Negus, V. E. 1949. The comparative anatomy and physiology of the larynx. New York, Hafner.

Peterson, G. and H. Barney. 1952. Control methods used in a study of the vowels. Journal of Acoustical Society of America. 24(2).175-84.

Schwartz, M. F. 1968. Identification of speaker sex from isolated, voiceless fricatives. Journal of Acoustical Society of America. 43.1178-79.

_____ and Helen Rine. 1968. Identification of speaker sex from isolated, whispered vowels. Journal of Acoustical Society of America. 44(6).1736-37.

Scott, J. P. 1958. Animal behavior. Chicago, University of Chicago Press.

Walker, G. F. and C. J. Kowalski. 1972. On the growth of the mandible. American Journal Phys. Anthro. 36.111-18.

STEREOTYPED ATTITUDES
OF SELECTED ENGLISH DIALECT COMMUNITIES

ROGER SHUY AND FREDERICK WILLIAMS

Georgetown University, University of Texas

Considerable evidence exists that just as research can reveal social stratification of various dialect features, it is also apparent that such stratification also exists in the subjective attitudes that persons have toward the dialects of others. Further, there is evidence that subjective judgments are not simply a unidimensional differentiation of social stratification, but are instead a multiple dimensional variety of connotative associations. That is, a person's reactions to a dialect may not only reflect his attitudes about the social stratum of that dialect, but may also include clusters of attitudes related to apparent qualities of the dialect or of the people who speak that dialect. Relative to the further study of these attitudes, one research question pertains to their dimensionality. A second refers to the generality of these dimensions among respondents from different ethnic groups and social strata, as well as according to sex. In the broadest sense, such attitudes, if they be defined, may begin to reveal the affective dimensions of dialect stereotyping.

The present report describes the results of a statistical analysis of subjective judgment data from an earlier study (Shuy, Baratz, and Wolfram 1969) which involved Detroit respondents' evaluations of five types of speech. The judgments were obtained as responses to five stimulus labels:

Detroit speech
White Southern speech

British speech
Negro speech
Standard speech

In the original design of the study, respondents had evaluated the speech concepts against selected semantic differential scales, each scale having adjectival opposites divided by seven steps, as follows:

Bad ___:___:___:___:___:___:___ Good

Results of the original analysis indicated selected reliable differentiations of the speech concepts in terms of individual scales; however, attention was not focused upon the dimensionality of such ratings, nor upon the use of those dimensions by different types of respondents. This paper reports a more detailed statistical analysis aimed at answering these questions.

Method

Respondents. Respondents reflected in the present data were the same as those described in the parent study (Shuy et al. 1969) who were selected from various elementary and high schools and adult groups in Detroit. The respondent sample (N = 620) incorporated four dimensions:

(1) Race: White (364), Black (256)
(2) Socioeconomic status: Upper middle (167), Lower middle (173), Upper working (140), and Lower working (140)[1]
(3) Age: 10-12 years old (286), 16-18 years old (170), and over 21 years old (164)
(4) Sex: Male (305) and Female (315)

Response scales. As an attempt to identify judgments presumably related to affective responses to the speech types, twelve semantic differential scales were selected from prior literature on the assumption that they reflected the connotative dimensions of judgment typically found in studies by Osgood and his associates (Osgood, Suci, and Tannenbaum 1957) and that they were, of course, relevant to speech attitudes. These dimensions of affective response are usually identified as 'evaluation', a person's 'good-bad' or 'pleasant-unpleasant' reaction to a stimulus; 'potency', the judged 'strength' of a stimulus, and 'activity', the perceived dynamic qualities of what is being judged. The scales selected for use were as follows:

dull	__:__:__:__:__:__:__	sharp
smart	__:__:__:__:__:__:__	dumb
weak	__:__:__:__:__:__:__	strong
fast	__:__:__:__:__:__:__	slow
complex	__:__:__:__:__:__:__	simple
worthless	__:__:__:__:__:__:__	valuable
good	__:__:__:__:__:__:__	bad
thin	__:__:__:__:__:__:__	thick[2]
careful	__:__:__:__:__:__:__	sloppy
rough	__:__:__:__:__:__:__	smooth
positive	__:__:__:__:__:__:__	negative
difficult	__:__:__:__:__:__:__	easy

Respondents recorded their reaction to stimulus labels by placing one checkmark on each scale, where the closer the checkmark is to a particular adjective, the more it indicates a greater association between the stimulus and that adjective. For purposes of numerical analysis, checkmarks are converted to a one-to-seven scale where the one is typically associated with the more positive adjective of the pair in each case.

Procedures. Response data for the different types of speech were gathered in the context of the larger study which had also involved a variety of ratings of tape recorded speech samples and a question- naire regarding respondent information. The details of this overall testing procedure can be seen in the report of the parent study (Shuy et al. 1969:5-22). Scales for each of the stimulus labels were random- ized so as to avoid order effects. Respondents were instructed to place one checkmark on each scale as an indication of their associ- ations between the scale and the concept.

Analyses and results

Dimensionality of ratings. The first question to be answered in the analyses was the degree to which the ratings reflected twelve relatively independent judgments which would correspond to each of the individual scales, as against groups of scales reflecting particular dimensions of judgment. If, as assumed at the outset, certain of the scales would reflect a 'good-bad' type of judgment, then it is likely that responses to scales such as 'positive-negative', 'valuable-worth- less', and the like would be highly interrelated. In other words, all such scales which reflected this type of evaluation would be sympto- matic of a single underlying dimension of evaluation. Similarly, it was expected that other scales such as would index potency and activity might cluster together to reflect more basic, underlying dimensions of judgment than characterized by the individual scales.

The degree to which scales were used in a way which reflected underlying dimensions of judgment was assessed by mathematical technique known as factor analysis. In general terms, factor analysis takes the interrelationships (intercorrelations) that have been found in the use of scales in rating the concepts, and mathematically defines hypothetical variables (factors) made up of clusters of scales which tend to have a high degree of interrelationship in usage. Here the mathematical solution of the factor analysis could be used to indicate the degree to which the interrelationships among the scales might define dimensions of evaluation (factors), and should also indicate which of the individual scales tend to contribute to those dimensions.

Results of the factor analysis[3] on the present data led to the identification of four factors characterizing interrelated use of scales. Based upon the identification of the scales contributing to them, the factors have been given labels to reflect overall dimensions of judgment of the speech types. These labels (or factors) and their respective scales were as follows:

Value: good-bad, positive-negative, smart-dumb, valuable-worthless, and smooth-rough.
Complexity: easy-difficult, simple-complex.
Potency: strong-weak, sharp-dull, and careful-sloppy.
Activity: fast-slow.

As anticipated in the initial selection of the scales, some of the affective dimensions of judgment as found in the studies by Osgood and his associates were again evident in evaluation of types of speech. The dimensions of 'activity' and 'potency' are directly identified among the above factors, and the label 'value' would be very closely associated with an evaluative dimension. There was, however, a further dimension which emerged in the present analysis; it was identified as a 'complexity' factor. In a theoretical sense, these results indicated that if respondents are given the response parameters defined by the earlier listed twelve scales, they will tend to subsume individual scales into four relatively general response dimensions. These dimensions correspond quite closely with the usual affective dimensions found in semantic differential research, but with the addition of a judgment apparently related to the perceived complexity of the type of speech. Because this dimension is separate from the evaluative dimension, it indicates that complexity is not presumed as neither particularly good nor bad. In a practical sense, these four dimensions can be used as a basis for differentiating respondents' attitudes toward the different types of speech judged in the study. Additionally, differences among the respondents themselves can be assessed in terms of the way these dimensions are used.

In order to make further comparisons among the speech types and the respondents' differences in use of the judgmental dimensions, ratings were averaged for scales contributing to each of the factors so as to provide 'factor scores'. These scores could range from one through seven, with one being positively associated with valuable, complex, potent, and active.

Stimulus differentiations. Given the conversion of respondents' individual scale markings to a set of factor scores corresponding to judgmental dimensions, it was then possible to undertake statistical analyses[4] to see how the four types of speech were differentiated relative to these dimensions of judgment. Figure 1 represents a summary

FIGURE 1. Average ratings of speech types on four judgmental dimensions.

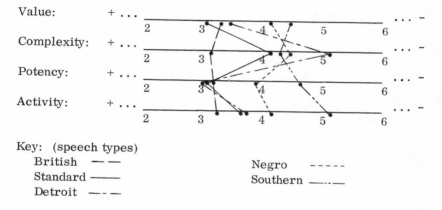

Key: (speech types)
British   — —
Standard ———
Detroit —–—

Negro   - - - - -
Southern —–··—

response profile of evaluations of the five types of speech relative to the four judgmental dimensions. In the broadest view the profiles showing the most similarity across different dimensions are those for ratings of Detroit speech and Standard speech, with the greatest difference being on the complexity dimension where Detroit speech was rated as less complex. Further, there appeared to be a gross and somewhat consistent differentiation of British speech as having relatively more positive ratings on all four dimensions as contrasted with Negro speech. Negro speech in turn had more positive ratings on all four dimensions than Southern speech, with the exception of ratings of complexity where the two did not significantly differ. In terms of tests of the statistical significance among mean differences, the following generalizations could be made:

(1) Value. Standard speech, British speech, and Detroit speech concepts were all rated as significantly more of value (and not different from one another), as compared with Negro speech, which in turn was rated as of greater average value than Southern speech.

(2) Complexity. British speech was rated as more complex than Standard speech, which was rated as slightly more complex than Southern and Negro speech (which were not different from each other), with Detroit speech being rated the least complex of all types.

(3) Potency. Detroit speech, British speech, and Standard speech were all rated as the most potent of the speech types, with no significant differences being found among these types. By contrast, Negro speech was judged as less potent as compared with these first types, and Southern speech significantly less potent than Negro speech.

(4) Activity. British speech was judged the most active of the speech types, followed by Standard speech and Detroit speech, which were not significantly different from each other. Negro speech was judged significantly less active than the first types, and this was followed by Southern speech which was judged the least active of all.

Interaction of respondent ethnicity and speech type. Results of overall statistical analysis indicated that a number of the generalizations about attitudes toward speech types would be necessarily modified according to the ethnicity of the respondent. These interactions were centered on three of the five types of speech being judged, namely, Southern, White, Negro, and Standard speech. By implication, the 'lack' of significant statistical interactions between ethnicity of respondent and ratings of Detroit and British speech indicate the generality of the findings for those two speech types across ethnic groups (as shown in Figure 1).

The speech type that resulted in the most interaction with ethnicity of respondent was that of Negro speech. Figure 2 summarizes the ethnic differences and average evaluations of Negro speech. As one might anticipate, the differences summarized in this figure indicate that blacks generally evaluate Negro speech in a more positive manner than do white respondents. The only reversal in this pattern is one in terms of complexity, where black respondents generally rate Negro speech as somewhat less complex. All such differences between the racial subgroups as shown in Figure 2 were statistically significant.

Beyond the above, there were further interactions on the value dimension that could be viewed as generally a counterpart of what is summarized in Figure 2. In the rating of Standard speech and Southern white speech, the average white ratings were more positive (2.95, 4.15) than were the average ratings by black respondents for these two

FIGURE 2. Average ratings of 'Negro speech' by black and white respondents.

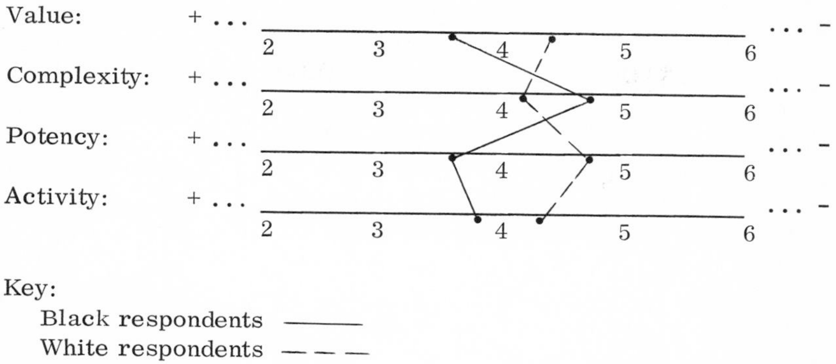

Value: + ... −
             2   3   4   5   6

Complexity: + ... −
             2   3   4   5   6

Potency: + ... −
             2   3   4   5   6

Activity: + ... −
             2   3   4   5   6

Key:
    Black respondents ————
    White respondents — — —

speech types (3.25, 4.70). In other words, just as black respondents tended to rate Negro speech more positively than did white respondents, the white respondents in turn rated Standard speech and Southern white speech as of more value than did the black respondents. The only other interaction between ethnicity of respondent and speech type occurred on the potency dimension, where white respondents rated Southern white speech more positively (4.38) than did black respondents (4.73).

Interaction of social status of the respondent and speech type. Only in terms of attitudes reflecting judgments on the value and potency dimensions were there interactions between the social class status of the respondent and judgments of the speech types. By implication, therefore, the results shown in Figure 1 for judgments of complexity and activity relative to the different speech types have generality across social status levels of the respondents.

Figure 3 summarizes the types of judgment where persons of different social status varied significantly in their average ratings. In terms of value judgments, the higher the social status of the individual, generally the more positively he regarded the value of British speech. A similar pattern was revealed for the rating of the potency of British speech. Here, again, the higher the social class of the respondent the more positively did he regard British speech. There were reversals of this order in terms of rating the potency of Detroit and of Negro speech. Here individuals in the lower social class tended to rate these two types of speech as more potent than did the higher class respondents. In the case of Detroit speech the ratings of the lowest social class were significantly more positive on potency than those of the other three groups, which were not significantly

FIGURE 3. Selected average ratings by respondents of different social status.

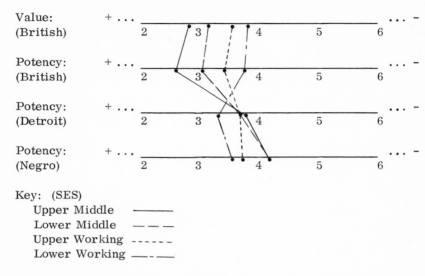

Key: (SES)
    Upper Middle   ————
    Lower Middle   — — —
    Upper Working   - - - - - -
    Lower Working   —·-·—

different from one another. Somewhat similar in the rating of potency of Negro speech, the two lower status groups gave the most positive ratings, as contrasted with the two higher social groups.

In all, the pattern seems to be that in rating a presumably prestigious form such as British speech, positiveness of rating will correspond with the higher the class level of the respondent. Conversely, for the everyday speech of Detroit, or the concept of Negro speech, the lower status individuals appear to rate these in a more positive manner relative to the potency dimension.

Interactions of age of respondent and speech type. On all judgmental dimensions, there were selected differences in average judgments of the speech types according to the age group of the respondent. The most revealing and interpretable of these differences was in terms of the various ratings by age groups of Standard speech. These are summarized in Figure 4 for ratings of value, complexity, and potency. The most evident pattern in Figure 4 is that adults tended to view standard speech as more positive in value and potency than did the two younger groups. At the same time, however, the two younger groups viewed Standard speech as more complex than did the adult groups. A roughly similar, although less salient, pattern appeared for ratings of British speech. Beyond these patterns, any further interactions between the age of the respondent and attitudes toward the speech type fit into no major nor interpretable pattern.

FIGURE 4.   Average ratings of 'Standard speech' by different age groups.

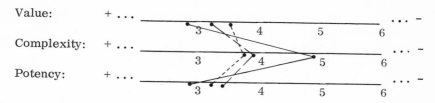

Key: (Age)
    Adult   ————
    16-18 years   — — —
    10-12 years   - - - - - -

Interactions of sex of respondent and speech type. In no case were there any statistically significant interactions between the sex of the respondent and variations in speech ratings. The implication here, then, was that the general patterns of speech evaluations as shown in Figure 1 prevailed across the male and female groups participating in this study.

Discussion

Summary. The main aims in the present analyses were (1) to determine the dimensionality of judgments yielded by Detroit respondents in rating selected types of speech, and (2) to determine the degree to which the judgments varied according to the respondents' ethnicity, social status, age, and sex. Results indicated that from a limited list of twelve semantic differential scales, four dimensions of judgment could be identified. These were labeled as 'value', 'complexity', 'potency', and 'activity'. In comparing judgments according to the different characteristics of respondents, the following results were obtained: There were reliable contrasts among ratings of the five different types of speech generally in the direction of rating Detroit speech and Standard speech in a roughly similar manner; rating British speech more positively on the four dimensions than Negro speech, and rating Negro speech more positively than Southern speech. Further, an interaction was found between the ethnicity of respondents and certain of the speech type judgments. This was mainly in the direction of black respondents rating Negro speech more positively on three of the four dimensions as compared with the average ratings by the white respondents. An interaction between social status of the respondent and speech attitudes indicated that higher status respondents tended to have more positive judgments of British speech in terms of both value and potency as compared to lower status respondents. The reverse seemed to be the case for evaluations of Detroit and Negro speech, where the lower-class respondents rated both in a more positive manner than did the higher-class respondents. An interaction of the age of respondent with speech attitude tended to indicate more positive ratings of standard speech and British speech by adults in terms of value and potency as compared with the ratings of the younger respondents. At the same time, however, the younger respondents rated standard speech as more complex than did the adults. Finally, there were no interactions between sex of respondents and speech attitudes, indicating that the overall attitudes found about speech characteristics had generality across sex.

Implications. Judgment dimensionality. Certainly it should be recognized that whatever dimensions of judgment are revealed in factor analytic studies such as this one are not only a function of the respondent's behaviors and the stimuli being judged, but are also constrained by the number and types of scales that are provided. That this list of scales was constructed with an eye toward the usual affective dimensions of evaluation potency, and activity, makes it no surprise that if dimensionality was to be found, dimensions similar to these emerged in the analysis. It is important to realize, however, that just because the scales may offer the potential for these factors, this does not guarantee that raters' behavior will be patterned accordingly. It is perfectly possible that persons could use each of the scales independently, hence there would be as many judgmental dimensions as there are scales; or, for that matter, persons could use all scales in a highly intercorrelated manner, thus yielding one global factor. What the present results reveal is that if the scales for the usual three dimensions are present in the evaluation situation, respondents will tend to use them in a manner somewhat reflective of the dimensions of value, potency, and activity. Beyond this, it appears that in assessment of language attitudes in this type of affective domain, a further dimension of complexity will be manifested.

These four dimensions can be contrasted with the two-dimensional model of 'confidence-eagerness' and 'ethnicity-nonstandardness' that has been found in a number of studies (cf. Williams 1970; Williams, Whitehead, and Miller 1972). These two dimensions were identified from adjectival scales that were initially developed from the respondent population themselves, in this case teachers. By analyzing a variety of teachers' open-ended descriptions about children and their speech, constructing scales from these adjectives, then by subsequent factor analytic work, it was revealed that teachers' evaluations were typically in terms of 'confidence-eagerness' and 'ethnicity-nonstandardness' judgments. These dimensions, it is thought, reflect a more pragmatic level of speech assessment, where a person's ratings are more directly tied to assessments of the speech and the speaker himself. By contrast, the more connotative-laden dimensions of value and the like reflect a much more subjective and affective reaction to speech characteristics and speakers. The two sets of judgmental dimensions, then, are not necessarily in conflict with one another, but represent different levels of a person's reaction to speech.

That the different speech types were reliably and interpretably differentiated along these four dimensions, is evidence that the dimensions reflect some level of psychological reality of stereotype attitudes of the respondents. These stereotype attitudes may be the other side of the social dialect coin in the sense that just as we may objectively classify the speech types assessed in this study, we may also expect to find persons' attitudes similarly differentiated among these types. In other words, dialect may have an objective reality in the way people talk, but it seems quite clear that it at the same time has a subjective reality in the kinds of consistent attitudes which people hold toward one another's speech. These kinds of attitudes are probably as important a part of the sociolinguistic picture as the objective data which we find in speech corpora.

NOTES

[1] Socioeconomic status categories were defined as follows: 'upper middle', college graduate usually with graduate training, dentist, mechanical engineer, personnel manager; 'lower middle', high school graduate, probably some college or technical school, printer, post office clerk, small business owner or manager; 'upper working', some high school, high school graduate, bus driver, carpenter, telephone line man; and 'lower working', not beyond eighth grade, dishwasher, night watchman, or construction laborer.

[2] Because of evidence in the parent study of the ambiguity of the 'thick-thin' scale, it was omitted from these analyses.

[3] In order to conserve space, the technical details of the analysis are not presented here. The model was a principal component solution, assuming perfect reliability of the scales, and rotating the resulting factor matrix according to varimax criteria.

[4] The main analysis model was a 4x2x4x2 analysis of variance having dimensions corresponding to speech types, respondent ethnicity, social status, and sex. This analysis was conducted once for each dependent variable, each of which was one of the four factor scores. Individual mean comparisons are made by Duncan range tests, with statistical significance interpreted at the $p < .05$ level.

96 / ROGER SHUY AND FREDERICK WILLIAMS

REFERENCES

Osgood, Charles E., George J. Suci, and Percy H. Tannenbaum.
1957. The measurement of meaning. Urbana, Ill., University
of Illinois Press.
Shuy, Roger W., Joan C. Baratz, and Walter Wolfram. Socio-
linguistic factors in speech identification. Project Report No.
MH 15048-01, National Institute of Mental Health.
Williams, Frederick. 1970. Psychological correlates of speech
characteristics: on sounding 'disadvantaged'. Journal of Speech
and Hearing Research. 13.472-88.
_____, Jack L. Whitehead, and Leslie M. Miller. 1972. (In press)
Relations between language attitudes and teacher expectancy.
American Educational Research Journal.

LANGUAGE, SPEECH AND IDEOLOGY: A CONCEPTUAL FRAMEWORK

DAVID M. SMITH

Georgetown University

1. Introduction. Most recent publication in the area of language attitudes has dealt with the problems of hearers' evaluating, grouping, and ranking speakers on the basis of speech. Several assumptions, some of which have been quite clearly demonstrated to be valid, appear to underlie the efforts to isolate these attitudes. It is now, for example, quite readily accepted that speech differences directly correlate with a number of social groupings and may, indeed, be among the major indicators of the social slots an individual fills.

It is also assumed that there exists a direct concomitant, if not causal, relationship between attitudes and behavior in that how one evaluates the speech of another person will have an effect upon how he acts toward that person. Of course, the effect does not stop here. Given the importance of communication in interpersonal relationships and the feedback-adjustive processes in communication, all parties to the communication event are eventually affected and attitude then becomes one of the primary determinants of the nature of the event (cf. Watzlawick et al. 1967).

It follows from this assumption, from the standpoint of the pragmatics of communication, that change in behavior will inevitably be attended by change in attitude. Whether the most 'practical' and 'workable' means to accomplish change, therefore, is to force behavior change and thus create dissonance necessitating a change in attitude, or to change attitude (perhaps by pointing out existing dissonance) is a debatable question. Both approaches are now being

97

advocated with respect to social behavior in a number of problem areas (Rokeach 1971).

The purpose of this paper is not to attempt a resolution of this pragmatic problem, in the sense of advocating one approach over another, but to attempt to tie together, within the matrix of culture, some of the concepts being dealt with. The orientation of this paper is, therefore, programmatic and theoretical rather than pragmatic and data-based. In it I hope to suggest a conceptual framework within which the results of existing research may be viewed to reveal relationships and lacunae which have practical significance.

2. The socio-cultural system. This section outlines in barest form the model of the socio-cultural system underlying the rest of the discussion. The general features of this model are illustrated in Figure 1. Not all of the features of the model included in the illustration are directly germane to the present discussion and so, in the interests of economy, will not be explained. The model in its entirety is presented to provide an easy fix on the ontological status of the concepts dealt with in more detail.

FIGURE 1. Schematic representation of the socio-cultural system.

Society	Societal groups	Individual	Manifestations	
Culture	Subculture	Personality	Behavior	Cult. Institutions[1]
Language[3]	Dialect	Idiolect	Linguistic behavior[2]	languages, kinesic systems, etc.
Ideolog. system	Groups of beliefs	Beliefs/ values	Esthetic/ ethical[2]	religions, art, prejudices
Social system	Social groups	Statuses	Inter-personal[2]	social organization
Techno. system	Groups of skills	Ind. skills/ techniques	Survival behavior[2]	Technology

[1] The term 'cultural institution', as with a number of other terms in this model, is used with a somewhat special sense, as the discussion will make clear.

[2] These all refer to modes of behavior.

[3] Lines 3, 4, 5, and 6 represent subsystems of the culture, hence the double line between lines 3 and 2.

In working with this model and its schematic representation, several facts should be kept in mind: (1) The model serves as a conceptual framework only; that is, it is a construct belonging to the world of conceptual reality. (2) While the model can be fruitfully used to explain empirical data, there is no necessary, direct,

isomorphic relationship existing between the concepts of the framework and discrete empirical phenomena. This is of course true of
any model; and, in fact, if it were not so would vitiate one of the main
advantages of such an approach. Thus, for example, while it might
be difficult or impossible to decide empirically whether any single
human behavior is ethological or cultural, it may still, for certain
purposes, be valuable to maintain the conceptual distinction. (3) No
strong mentalistic or supraorganic claims are made concerning the
nature of this construct; for the present, it is suggested as a useful
heuristic device with clear explanatory value.

    2.1 Society/culture. While, with the exception of the Language
and the Ideological systems, no detailed description of the nature of
the particular concepts here presented will be offered, there are
several general concepts which must be carefully distinguished from
one another. One such distinction, often overlooked, or at least not
consistently explicated by linguists, is that between society and culture. Although for many purposes they may be considered coterminous
and equivalent, when dealing with language and with attitudes it is important to keep them conceptually distinct.
    Society here refers to systems of organisms, while 'culture' may
be defined simply as the learned system of rules which governs the
behavior of the members of a society. The many implications of this
distinction for the nature of society are treated in any good introduc-
tory textbook on cultural anthropology, and so need not be discussed
here. (Cf. especially Bock 1969, on whose analysis the above model
is based.) One point of extreme significance, however, must be made
at this juncture. This kind of dichotomy embodies a technical, i.e.
one way, implication. The presence of a society (or of an individual)
does not imply the presence of a culture (or of a personality). However, a culture or a personality system, obviously, cannot exist
apart from a society. Therefore, ideally it is possible to posit the
following society-culture possible combinations with respect to
species of living organisms.

    +Society/+Culture (+S/+C)
    +Society/-Culture (+S/-C)
    -Society/-Culture (-S/-C)

Of course, these are representations of polar extremes and it is
probable that species have degrees of culture or are more or less
social. This actual empirical reality could best be depicted on a continuum and translation to the kind of digital representation shown
above would require assigning values to points on the continuum.
However, even this does not vitiate the importance of the distinctions

here alluded to. The clearest example of +S/+C is the human species, while +S/-C characterizes the infrahuman social species.

The implications of this relationship between society and culture for communication theory in general are many and are particularly significant for the study of language attitudes. For example, in human society, the +S/+C type communication involves not only the transfer of information between individuals, but between individuals with personalities. Personality systems are cultural and are a function of the interplay of Language, the Social System, the Ideological and Technological systems. The significance of this will emerge more explicitly below.

2.11 Cultural/ethological. Recognizing a basic distinction between culture and society and the fact that society does not necessarily imply culture, requires the positing of a noncultural mechanism for meeting the social imperatives in +S/-C configurations. Traditional anthropology has subsumed the study of infrahuman social behavior under the rubric of ethology. I will use the term 'ethological' in keeping with this traditional usage, with reference to behavior patterns whose basis is a function of human genetics, i. e. that is, behavior which is shared although innate and not learned.

While it is empirically impossible to easily distinguish between behaviors which are culturally and ethologically based, any discussion of language attitudes must recognize this distinction. Indeed, much of the furor over the Bereiter, Englemann, Jensen, Herrnstein et al. positions regarding human intelligence stems from a lack of clear consensus as to what roles culture and ethology play in human behavior.

The present paper in no way pretends to suggest a solution to this problem, but it does attempt to provide a conceptual framework within which the problem can be approached. Both Language and Ideology (as well as their manifestations, languages, and attitudes) are viewed as cultural phenomena. However, it is recognized that they are both based in the genetic makeup of the human animal so that, just as all humans are provided at birth with an innate set of strategies for creating behavioral symbols, thus making language of a specific type inevitable, so we can assume systems of beliefs, values, and attitudes with their attendent behaviors will be universal and inevitable. While distinguishing culturally from ethologically based behavior is not central to the thrust of this paper, this distinction is nonetheless essential to an understanding of the theoretical framework here adduced.

2.12 Individual/collective. One other feature of Figure 1 should be explained; that is, the significance of the concepts listed in the horizontal rows and the significance of their arrangement. On each line the item in the third column represents the smallest unit of the entity on the left. However, the relationship is not simply that of a whole composed of discrete parts. While society, as I have defined it, is composed of groups (called societal groups to distinguish them from social groups) which are composed of individuals, the individual can be a member of more than one group. Furthermore, while a culture can be seen as the sum total of its subcultures, any personality system shares in a number of subcultures.

This schema throws into vivid relief a problem that is important in a number of fields but which is of particular practical interest to modern linguists. I refer to the question of the meaning of 'dialect'. As the term is used in the literature it can refer to either a group of isolects or a group of idiolects. In either case, 'dialect' tends to refer to a fiction or ideal. The problematicality of the concept as to its empirical validation has been an impetus to the development of variation theory in linguistics. It is noteworthy that parallel developments have been reported in genetics where modern, physical anthropologists find the popular concept race, like that of dialect, and for the same reasons, problematic (cf. Harris 1971:87-105). This has led to positing more useful models of genetic variation, focusing on the traits themselves rather than their biological loci. Something of the same sort has also been developing in the field of personality theory where theorists are focusing increasingly on personality traits as manifest in relationships rather than on personalities as monads. (Cf. for example Laing 1967, Watzlawick et al. 1967.)

2.2 Culture/behavior. Basic to the socio-cultural approach advocated here is the distinction between culture and behavior. Behavior is viewed as the activities of individuals which may exhibit patterning, either because it has a shared cultural or ethological base. Culture and the various subsystems of culture are viewed as sets of rules. While this approach is not at all new, careful observance of this distinction has several important implications. First, a number of things which are often subsumed under the general term 'culture' are seen in new relationships. Thus, speech is seen as a mode of cultural behavior, a direct output of the Language, but at the same time only one mode of a behavior event which has at the same time a direct output relationship with the Ideological and other culture systems. Specific language codes, like religions or governments, are here considered the end products of the rules which underlie them, and are thus given a basis for a new kind of comparability.

Before turning to a more detailed consideration of the two culture systems being discussed here, one further observation is in order. The representative concepts listed in the last two columns of Figure 1 constitute the data for ethnographic efforts (including descriptive linguistics). The object of such descriptions is, of course, that of abstracting the rules. This schema should indicate clearly the problems inherent in doing one type of ethnography, writing the grammar of a language, for example, without considering the other aspects of culture.

3. Language. In this section the components, manifestations, and functions of Language as a cultural system are sketched. Throughout the paper the word 'language' is used in two technically different senses. Language (with a capital 'L') denotes the set of cultural rules which engenders not only speech but other nonverbal linguistic behavior as well. In the area of manifestation, language (with a lower case 'l') is used with reference to the particular linguistic code the behavior results in. The distinction is close to that of competence/performance, although performance would have to be expanded to include nonverbal behavior as well as verbal (a distinction which on close scrutiny becomes rather arbitrary in any case).

The significance of keeping the ontological status of these concepts firmly fixed is that only then can a model be produced which is amenable to meaningful comparison. Thus, Language enjoys the same conceptual status as Ideological System, and likewise a language that of a kinesic system, a proxemic system, or a religious organization of the same subculture.

3.1 The components. Figure 2 is provided as a schematic model of Language. While it looks suspiciously like a stratificational model, closer inspection will reveal that it is intended to be no more than a very general attempt to depict several important features of Language relative to its status as a cultural system. This paper is not designed to describe the nature of the components or their relationship to each other. That, of course, is the task of theoretical linguistics.

FIGURE 2. Language as a culture system.[1]

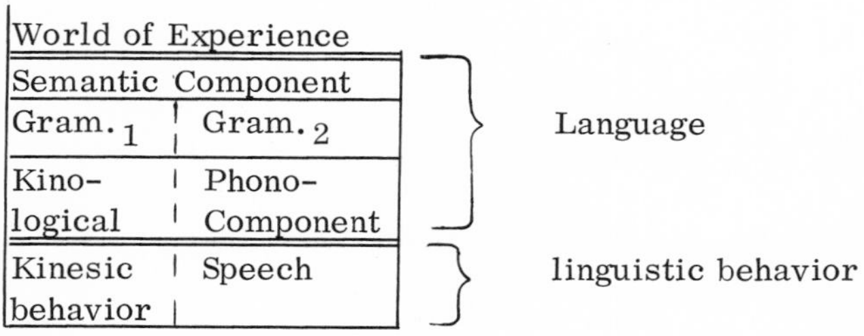

Several notions relevant to the present discussion are illustrated here. First, Language is viewed as a subset of cultural rules designed to create symbols. It is a coding device which has the property of enabling a person to engage in behaviors which will be considered meaningful by other members of the same society or societal group. As such it must have a component which stands in some kind of isomorphic relationship to an actor's conceptualization of the world of reality he experiences. This, in Figure 2, has been labeled the semantic component, but the actual translation of this concept into a model of language will depend upon individual orientation. (While not of primary concern here, this general model appears to suggest a de facto equation of deep structure with the semantic component in generative terminology.)

The grammatical and phonological components need not be discussed except to point out that this definition of Language is expanded to account for all linguistic behavior and thus, a complication is added to these two components. They must contain the rules generating nonverbal linguistic behavior as well as speech. In Figure 2 this is recognized by dividing the grammatical and phonological components into two parts and referring to them as $gram_1$, $gram_2$, kinological, and phonological. This is, of course, a purely conventional and inadequate technique, since an adequate model would have to be much more complex (see note 1). The term 'kinesic' is used in a technical sense to include any behavior produced, consciously or unconsciously, resulting from the application of a set of Language rules which serve to equate it (the behavior) with a conceptualized universe.

3.2 Manifestations. Focusing on the behavioral manifestations of Language, several implications for this model need explicating. First, I am suggesting that all linguistic behavior be considered based on a single semantic component. This is not to say that all semantic concepts can be expressed equally well verbally or kinesically, or that all semantic concepts are even viewed by a speaker as expressable both ways. This type of judgment is largely a function of individual enculturation and/or competence. However, this view does serve to tie the two modes of linguistic behavior together in a suggestively fruitful way.

Second, the two modes of linguistic behavior alluded to here are not only distinguished by the parts of anatomy used in their production or the channels utilized (which turn out to be rather arbitrary anyway) but more importantly by certain design features. That is, kinesic behavior appears more analogic while speech more digital. This availability of two modes of linguistic behavior, which can be produced simultaneously, has long been recognized as conferring significant adaptive advantage on humans. All that is suggested here is that, given the difference in the nature of the two outputs, we should expect some semantic concepts would be viewed by speakers as intrinsically more easily expressed in one mode than the other. (For example, things viewed as standing in continua-type relationships might be more easily conceived as expressed kinesically.)

A final implication for this model concerns the practical problem of analysis. Since kinesic and speech behavior are based on different operational principles, their respective analyses should consequently call for different sets of techniques and the tool kit developed for speech analysis will not be totally effective in kinesic analysis. Furthermore, if the two types of behavior are products of the same underlying system, it would be reasonable to expect that they will both have ethological and cultural bases of the same sorts. If it is assumed that there are universals in the deep structure of language, we should also expect universals to be reflected in kinesic systems.

3.3 The functions of Language. This short discussion of the components and manifestations of Language has been intended to pave the way for a discussion of its functions. The position taken here is that once a society, or a member of a society, has at his disposal a cultural mechanism, in this case a language or a kinesic system, it is free to use that mechanism to meet a variety of needs. With respect to both Language and Ideological Systems, these functions can be viewed as being of two types, the intrinsic and the social.

3.31 The referential function. The intrinsic or linguistic function of language has been called its referential function (Hymes 1968:117 ff). By referential function, I mean the process just described, that of relating in a systematic way specific behaviors to conceptualized aspects of the world of experience. The design features basic to natural language permit the efficient accomplishment of this.

3.32 The social functions. The social functions of language alluded to here have been described in some detail elsewhere (Smith 1972). They include the communicative, the expressive, and the integrative. The communicative function refers to the transmission of information between personalities. This can be viewed as the primary social function, so that the other functions must either make use of features designed to accomplish this function or develop characteristics which will not interfere with communication. The integrative function is the use of language in tying individuals into the social system of a society. Basically the amenability of language to this function rests on its intrinsic variability, and it is no accident that developments in variation theory were stimulated by attempts to explain the integrative function of language. The expressive function refers to the use of language to express the particular cognitive orientation of an individual or a societal group by linguistic behavior.

Two facts emerge as significant here. First, each of the social functions is directly predicated upon language performing its referential function. Communication can only take place when participants to the communication event share the same coding apparatus. Integration is based on the peculiar nature of the coding apparatus since the intrinsic nature of language permits the saying of the same thing in different ways. Therefore, how one says something (verbally and/or nonverbally), as well as what one chooses to talk about, can be used to mark social identity. In the same manner, the expressive function is possible precisely because language, as a referential device, provides a way for symbolizing a cognitive orientation.

Second, it must be remembered that any speech event will, in all probability, be used to accomplish all of these functions simultaneously. This means that just as any specific cultural behavior can be viewed at one and the same time as the output of all the cultural systems, so any speech event can be viewed as meeting all three of these social needs.

4. Ideological systems. Having sketched the components, the manifestations, and functions of Language, only brief allusion will be made here to parallels in the Ideological System. The Ideological System is the set of rules which an individual has acquired for making judgments about things or behaviors he experiences. Therefore, it is the culture system that engenders what can be termed esthetic or ethical modes of behavior. A speech act, to give an example, while always performed according to the rules of the Language, is also judged by both speaker and hearer(s) as more or less good, proper, appropriate, etc. These judgments are ordinarily made in context of the other culture systems; for example, 'Is the speech act good or appropriate given the social identity of the speaker and hearer?' 'Is it esthetic for the social context and genre?'

Of course, as with the other rules of society, there is individual and group variation in the ideological rules. Explicating these rules and their patterns of variation is a significant, implication-fraught, ethnographic problem.

4.1 Components of the Ideological system. The type of model suggested for Language can be used to represent the Ideological system (cf. Figure 3). This does not suggest that the internal components of Language and Ideology are in any way equivalent or that they perform the same referential functions.

What they do have in common is that both culture systems provide sets of rules for relating a conceptualization of the world of experience

FIGURE 3. Schematic model of the Ideological system.

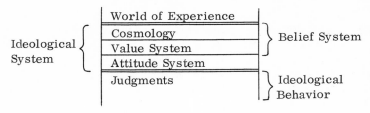

to behavior. In the case of the Ideological system, this component can be termed, to slightly redefine a well-tested term, the cosmology. The cosmology of a person, societal group, or society is the set of beliefs concerning how things are. Moving toward behavior, an Ideological system also provides a component spelling out how things should be; this is the value system. (Traditionally, these two components together have been considered the belief system.)

Finally, the Ideological system contains a component which serves to arrange and relate values and beliefs to each other and to behavior; this is the system of attitudes. Put in other words, the cosmology, a set of beliefs concerning the world of experience, is realized as a value system, which indicates how things should be. This in turn is realized as a set of attitudes which is realized behaviorally as a set of esthetic-ethical judgments.

4.2 Manifestations of the Ideological system. Due to the rather speculative nature of the model sketched here, only a few very tentative suggestions are tendered as to the manifestations. The rules concerning how things are and should be with respect to various segments of experience are often explicitly formulated and woven into some kind of system which then has typical behavioral and physical manifestation.

For example, beliefs concerning the supernatural are sometimes organized into religious systems. As with languages, most of the religious system may either be shared by all of society, or only by very small segments.

Another example is to be found in art traditions. A particular school of art will be based on a shared set of beliefs concerning what is beautiful, good technique, etc. These rules give rise to characteristic behaviors and are manifest as art forms. Significantly, not only will the appreciation of the art form by the public be a function of the amount of sharedness of the Ideological system; but also, since artistic behavior is also symbolic, this appreciation will depend on the degree to which it is the result of a shared Language. The same can be said for religious systems. This simply further demonstrates that all behavior ultimately has to be recognized as the product of all of culture.

These examples are the clearest illustrations of the manifestations of the Ideological system because in the case of religion and art we have features of the Ideological system used as criteria in defining subcultures. There are, of course, many other manifestations, such as prejudices and stereotypes, which are not as explicitly recognized and which are not as neatly coterminous with subculture boundaries.

4.3 Functions of the Ideological system. The previous statement leads directly to a consideration of the functions of the Ideological system. As already noted, the intrinsic (again, the term 'referential' also seems appropriate) function of the Ideological system is to provide a set of rules whereby an individual may make judgments about his world of experience. The social functions are based on this fact and are of primary importance here.

As with our discussion of Language, we must start with the manifestations of the rules; that is, the ethos, eidos, religious systems, etc. In section 4, the inherent variability in the rules of the Ideological system was noted. This is of critical significance, since I suggest that the primary social function of the ideology is integration. Again, integration is defined as the tying of individuals into the social system. Ideology performs this in several ways. First, because of its intrinsic function of establishing standards of judgment, ideology provides a set of sanctions. The exact nature of these sanctions will depend on the nature of the beliefs and values themselves. Second, due to the variation exhibited in the ideological behavior of individuals, a basis for marking individuals as members of a social group is made available. (This process rests on a fact that has been implicit in all of the discussion to this point; namely, that a Society is free to use any discernible difference in behavior or physical characteristics as attributes of membership in a social group. Examples of the latter are skin color, age, sex, and biological relationship. Examples of the former include speech differences, religious behavior, and homosexuality. Obviously positing a biological trait as criterial to social group membership will lead to concomitant behavioral differences as well.)

Even though the primary social function of the Ideological system and its manifestations may be considered integrative, it also performs other functions. Since for the individual the rules relate behavior to the world of experience the individual has another mechanism for expressing his cognitive orientation. Indeed, any cultural behavior expresses a set of values and beliefs. Furthermore, it can be easily demonstrated that manifestations of the ideology are also used communicatively.

At this point a potentially interesting notion suggests itself. If the primary social function of Language is to provide mechanisms of communication and if the primary social function of the Ideological system is to provide integrative mechanisms, these differential functional loads should have implications for the basic nature of the systems. One thing that comes to mind is the kind of variation permitted. It would seem logical that there would be stronger constraints on permissible variation in the Language. This is, of course, assuming that communicative efficiency is directly proportional to the amount of sharedness of the rules which engenders the behavior in a way not true for integrative adequacy. Whether or not this suggests a fruitful paradigm for ethnographic investigation remains to be seen.

5. The relationship between Language and the Ideological system.

5.1 The cultural nature of the systems. The most obvious way in which Ideological systems and Languages are related is that they are both culture systems with all of the attributes of such systems. This means; for example, that they are adaptive, learned, conventional, and largely unconscious.

All of culture is ultimately adaptive. It is, from the societal, subsocietal, and individual viewpoint, an integrated set of rules which is essential to survival. While demonstrating the validity of this claim is fairly easy, it is beyond the scope of our interest here. However, from a practical point of view, one implication is important, for it has been painfully pressed upon any of us who are concerned with behavior change. Emotional commitment to established patterns of behavior is apt to be profound, not just because of some ethnocentric notion that this is the only, or best way to do something, but because doing it this way has important survival value. It, therefore, becomes incumbent upon the culture-change broker to demonstrate that his suggested changes will not jeopardize the survival of those who are being asked to change. (This is often difficult precisely because changes induced, for the most commendable reasons, have too often, in fact, proved ultimately lethal.)

Thus, for example, one must be convinced that changing his attitude toward a particular type of speech will not have repercussions he cannot handle. If, on the other hand, change in linguistic behavior is proposed, the speaker must also be convinced that his change will not result in the release of unpleasant sanctions by the system in which he is operating due to his violation of the rules of the Ideological system. Fear of upsetting this delicate balance, and consequently of losing the 'adaptive' edge is at the root of much of the opposition to language and language attitude change being marketed today.

It would also appear that the cultural model of the Ideological system sketched here holds clues as to what is the least traumatic avenue to behavior change. Rather than force behavior change, which produces dissonance in the system that then has to be resolved, the alternative, that of pointing out, where possible, existing dissonances and bringing them to the consciousness, would result in less trauma to the system. For example, Rokeach (1971) has had apparently good results in changing attitudes toward race by pointing out in an experimental context conflicts in peoples' attitude system that already exist with respect to this issue.

Another implication of the cultural status of these two systems involves the individual. The Ideological system and its manifestations are seen as standing in the same relationship to the individual as is language. That is, the individual is at the same time, the matrix for cultural behavior, the locus of the rules, and a participant in a system of rules which is larger than himself. Thus, with regard to ideological behavior, the individual is, as with language, both a victim of the system and its creator.

5.2 The same relationship to reality. Another interesting area of relationship between Ideology and Language which becomes clear from this approach is the close affinity between what I have called cosmology and the semantic component. It little matters whether we use the term 'world view', which is usually reserved for language, or 'cosmology' which is usually associated with ideology, to express the relationship between the systems under consideration and the world of experience. For a given culture, subculture, or personality the two are identical. Thus, we see that what has been considered to be, for heuristic purposes, two distinct though interrelated systems are, in fact, interpenetrating. This is significant in at least the following two respects.

5.21 Judgments as linguistic symbols. Judgments, which are seen as the behavioral realizations of ideological rules, become a part of the world of experience of a speaker. They must, therefore, be amenable to linguistic symbolization in the semantic component, and through the application of the grammatical and kino-/phono-logical rules have behavior realizations. Thus, once judgments are made, the language has to provide a means for expressing the judgment linguistically.

5.22 Speech as part of the cosmology. On the other hand, linguistic behavior, by the same token, becomes automatically an element in the experience of a participant in the behavior. From the viewpoint of the Ideological system, therefore, this must be accounted for in the belief, value, and attitude system so that a judgment can be made about it.

The implications for this are at the same time rather profound. Any behavior, whether viewed from the perspective of Language or Ideology, and more particularly behavior outside the range of the expected, is ultimately going to have effect on the view of reality embodied in the culture. This is true not only for that particular view held by the individual participants in the behavior event, but ultimately for the system as a whole. To put it another way, any change in attitude, and thus judgment, is going to result in semantic change; any change in speech patterns is going to result eventually in change in belief systems.

5.3 Both subject to the same kinds of variation. Allusion has been made to the effects variation theory has had in genetics, linguistics, and personality theory. It would seem to follow from the sketch presented here, that some similar advantages would accrue if the principles of variation theory were applied to an understanding of attitudes. The matter of stereotyping particularly suggests itself at this point.

Recent studies by Williams (1971) have indicated some interesting demonstrations of the accuracy of stereotypes as regards speech behavior. In light of the discussion in section 5.2 of the interpenetrating nature of the Ideological system and Language, this would be expected. In fact, stereotyping comes close to being a self-fulfilling prophecy in a clearly understandable way, people do act according to the stereotype since the stereotype is the way they act. However, if we shift our attention from the individual, to the individual attitudinal traits themselves, which are present in many people with different manifestations and in different combinations, we get a different picture as to how the system works. In other words, the same type of salutatory effects afforded by a shift from idiolect or dialect to lect in linguistics might result.

To make this more specific, getting people to focus on lectal phenomena (read specific behavioral traits), rather than stereotypes, could have the effect of pointing out cognitive dissonance, thus facilitating the kind of behavior change suggested in section 5.1. That is, the presence of a specific behavioral trait does not define a personality type; indeed, the judger himself probably exhibits the same behavior in different ways.

6. Conclusion. The above has been a rather speculative attempt to sketch, from the perspective of a cultural anthropologist, a sociocultural framework that depicts the relationship between Language, speech, and attitudes--concepts critical to sociolinguistics. In doing this, I have expanded the generally held notion of Language and have

posited a parallel culture system which is interrelated and inter-penetrating with Language. This I have termed the Ideological system. This stands in the same relationship to culture in general, the individual, society, and behavior as does Language. Attitudes are posited as comprising a system component of the Ideological system. Therefore, they are directly related to judgments (ideological behavior) as the components of Language are to speech.

This framework is adduced as a step in developing a unified paradigm for looking at these various phenomena, which, it becomes increasingly apparent, are closely interrelated, both systematically and functionally. Whether or not the effort is of value remains largely an ethnographic problem.

NOTE

[1]The diagram in Figure 2 is only representative. It shows two grammars, $Gram_1$ and $Gram_2$. To be complete it would have to provide for at least four outputs and would have to show an equal number of grammars. The outputs would be speech, kinesic, proxemic, and paralinguistic codes.

REFERENCES

These references are limited to sources actually alluded to in the paper.

Birdwhistell, Ray. 1970. Kinesics and context. Philadelphia, University of Pennsylvania Press.
Bock, Philip K. 1969. Modern cultural anthropology: an introduction. New York, Alfred A. Knopf.
Harris, Marvin. 1971. Culture man and nature: an introduction to general anthropology. New York, Thomas Y. Crowell Co.
Hymes, Dell. 1964. Toward ethnographies of communication. In: The ethnography of communication. Ed. by John Gumperz and Dell Hymes. American Anthropologist. December 1964.
_____. 1968. The ethnography of speaking. In: Readings in the sociology of language. Ed. by Joshua Fishman. The Hague, Mouton.
Laing, Ronald D. 1967. The politics of experience. New York, Pantheon Books.
Rokeach, Milton. 1971. Persuasion that persists. Psychology Today. September 1971.
Smith, David M. 1972. Language as social adaptation. Languages and Linguistics: Working Papers, Number 4. Washington, D.C., Georgetown University Press.

Watzlawick, Paul, Janet Beavin, and Donald Jackson. 1967. The pragmatics of human communication: a study of interactive patterns, pathologies and paradoxes. New York, Norton.

Williams, Frederick. 1971. Some recent studies of language attitudes. Paper presented to Georgetown University faculty forum. October 21.

SOME RESEARCH NOTES ON DIALECT ATTITUDES AND STEREOTYPES

FREDERICK WILLIAMS

The University of Texas

The point has already been made by a number of researchers e.g. Labov 1966, Shuy 1969, Williams 1970a) that linguistic attitudes are the other side of the social dialect coin. That is to say, if we have language features that are known to be correlated with the social stratification of speakers, then it seems plausible--and research has borne out--that such features may serve as cues in the listener's estimate of a speaker's social status. To date most studies in this area have placed the emphasis upon linguistic variables, or the features which are socially stratified, and how these variables may serve in attitudinal evaluations by listeners. In contrast, the aim of the present study is to examine some aspects of the attitudinal processes presumed to operate when persons make such judgments. Specific attention is given to the concept of social dialect stereotypes. My thesis is that, to varying degrees, persons have a stereotyped set of attitudes about social dialects and their speakers and these attitudes play a role in how a person perceives the cues in another person's speech. This paper (1) reviews a method for determining and measuring attitudes that some populations of teachers have reflected in their evaluations of children's speech, (2) summarizes how these measurements have been used to define operationally dialect stereotypes, and finally, (3) presents speculations on how the dialect stereotypes appear to enter into the processes of speech evaluations.

Attitude measurement. The chief measurement technique in the present series of studies is known as 'semantic differential' scaling. Typically a semantic differential scale involves the evaluation of a concept or stimulus by rating it on scales comprised of adjectival opposites. Thus, for example, a person might rate a speech sample in terms of the following scale:

fast ___:___:___:___:___:___ slow

If the respondent thought that the speaker sounded either extremely fast or slow, he would place a check mark in one of the extreme cells of the scale. He could indicate a lesser degree of extremity by marking in either of the second most extreme positions; the adjective quite is often used to identify these two cells. If the respondent evaluated the speaker as either somewhat fast or somewhat slow, he would mark either of the cells adjacent to the center of the scale. Finally if the intended rating is neutral or no judgment, the center cell is checked (sometimes persons are allowed to indicate no judgment simply by not marking the scale).

By having sets of such scales, it is possible to have a respondent rate multiple attitudes toward a stimulus; for example:

Speaker A:

fast ___:___:___:___:___:___ slow
unclear ___:___:___:___:___:___ clear
fluent ___:___:___:___:___:___ not fluent

Numbers can be assigned to the cells of the scales so that it is possible to convert check-mark responses into quantitative data and hence to calculate descriptive or inferential statistics. If, for example, we mark these scales with the digits '1' through '7', associating the '1' with the more favorable adjective in each of the above pairs, we might calculate that a group of people rating Speaker A and Speaker B show the following contrasts in their average evaluations:

	Speaker A	Speaker B
fast--slow:	3.6	4.1
clear--unclear:	2.9	2.8
fluent--not fluent	1.8	2.3

Beyond using averages to describe these evaluations, we could see, for example, whether the differences between the mean ratings for Speakers A and B on each scale were greater than would be expected by chance alone. In other words we would have a statistical basis for seeing whether there are statistically significant differences in the way Speakers A and B are evaluated by a given group of people.

It is possible to derive semantic scales empirically from a respondent population, and this was done at several points in the studies (Williams 1970b; Williams, Whitehead, and Miller 1971a, 1972) reflected in this paper. Briefly, the technique was to present small groups of respondents with audiotape or videotape speech samples, then to get persons to comment freely upon their impressions about the samples. In these studies the respondents were teachers or student teachers and the language samples from school children. The teachers were asked to describe their opinions of how well the child did in school, what his educational background seemed like, and what his speech and language seemed like. From these discussions, it was possible to identify adjectives that teachers typically used in talking about the children as well as the particular referends to which these adjectives were applied. Some sample scales developed in this way, although in a format slightly modified from that just presented, include:

The child seems:
    hesitant ___:___:___:___:___:___:___ enthusiastic
The child sounds:
    tense ___:___:___:___:___:___:___ relaxed
The child's family is probably:
    low social status ___:___:___:___:___:___:___ high social status

At the first stages in the development of such scales, some fifty to sixty scales are usually prepared. Then by a program of pilot testing and various statistical methods used in scale development, it is possible to reduce the number of scales to those clusters of scales which seem to account for the most amount of differentiation among stimuli. Or, to put it more practically, scale development has allowed the identification of those clusters of scales that teachers seem to use the most in differentiating among different samples of children's speech.

In studies involving small groups of black and white teachers in Chicago (Williams 1970b), black and white teachers in Memphis (Williams and Shamo 1972), and black, white, and Mexican-American teachers in central Texas (Williams et al. 1971a, 1972; Williams, Whitehead, and Traupmann 1971) it has been found that two major clusters of scales account for the most amount of differentiation of children's speech samples. One of these clusters of scales has been made up of such adjective pairs as 'unsure--confident', 'active--passive', 'reticent--eager', and 'hesitant--enthusiastic'. Throughout the aforementioned studies clusters of this type have been interpreted as indexing an overall evaluation of a child's 'confidence-eagerness'. In other words, these scales taken together measure a global attitude by which the teachers differentiate children's speech. The subjective interpretation has been that evaluations on this dimension generally reflect the degree to which the child speaks continuously and fluently, carries the 'conversational ball' and reflects enthusiasm. Some objective evidence on this interpretation is that as the frequency of hesitation phenomena increases in speech samples, it can be mathematically demonstrated that the ratings of 'confidence-eagerness' tend to become more negative.

A second major cluster of scales found in the above studies was made up of such adjective pairs as 'standard American--marked ethnic style', 'White-like--non-white-like', 'low social status--high social status', and 'disadvantaged--advantaged'. This cluster in all of the preceding studies has been labeled as a broad evaluative dimension of 'ethnicity-nonstandardness'. Presumably evaluations on this dimension reflect the degree to which a child's speech characteristics are associated with low prestige markers, particular social status, or a particular ethnic group. It was found that to the degree that speech samples contained selected nonstandardizations (e. g. , d for th substitutions, pronominal apposition, etc.), the more that the same samples were rated as sounding ethnic-nonstandard.

In a practical sense, the development of the above scales has provided a measurement technique for eliciting and eventually quantifying attitudinal evaluations of children's speech. In a more theoretical sense, it has indicated that among groups of teachers there seems to be a global two-dimensional framework for evaluation. In many of the reports mentioned above, it has been speculated that these two evaluative dimensions may be a reflection of at least two major dimensions of variations found in social dialect studies. There is the differentiation of the child's grammar (i. e. his linguistic system as manifested in performance), and this may be reflected in ratings of ethnicity-nonstandardness. There are variations in the fluency of performance using a particular grammar and this may be reflected mainly in the gross evaluations of 'confidence-eagerness'.

The two-dimensional model of 'ethnicity-nonstandardness' and 'confidence-eagerness' lends itself well for use in plotting graphic summaries of differentiations that respondents may make among different children. Figure 1 presents a two-dimensional plot where the mean ratings of children on 'ethnicity-nonstandardness' and 'confidence-eagerness' scales have been calculated, and where averages have been plotted in a two-dimensional space. The ratings in this figure are from a pilot phase of the Chicago research and involved teachers' evaluations of middle and low status white and black

FIGURE 1. Example of the two-dimensional plot of mean ratings.

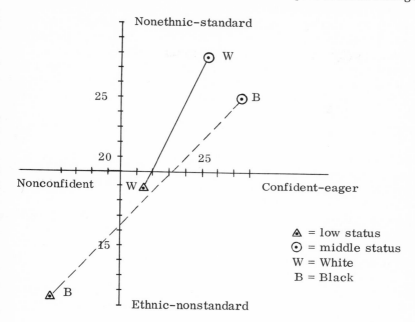

children. Each child had a set of ratings averaged across the respondents and the scales for each of the 'confidence-eagerness' and 'ethnicity-nonstandardness' dimensions. A point is then located on the diagram for the average ratings on these two dimensions for each of the stimuli. For example, the average ratings of middle class white children here were 27.5 on 'ethnicity-nonstandardness' and 25.2 in 'confidence-eagerness'. The intersection of those two coordinates in the two factor diagram defines the location of the plot for that stimulus. Note in Figure 1 how such plots provide for the simultaneous summary of the average ratings for the different stimuli on the two dimensions. Speaking more theoretically, we can say that the two-dimensional diagram is a model of the parameters of language or speech evaluation, at least in terms of the teacher populations studied.

The identification of stereotypes. The idea of measuring persons' stereotypes of particular dialects or speakers was arrived at in a somewhat backward way. A review of the literature of language evaluation studies (e.g. Shuy 1969) indicated that although some studies used very brief samples of speech (e.g. 3 to 10 seconds), it was often remarked that reliable ratings could be obtained with these samples.

In some unreported pilot studies by the present researcher, it was found that respondents would willingly fill in the rating scales not only for very short samples of speech but would also fill them in when simply told of a particular type of child who was to speak and where no tape was presented as a stimulus. This prompted the assumption that respondents were prone to employ an anticipation of attitudes (psychological set) toward a particular type of child and that these attitudes, if not prompted by a description of some type, would be elicited by the first relevant cues heard (or seen) in stimulus presentation. Such attitudes were assumed to reflect a 'stereotype'. The question, then, was what relation these stereotype attitudes had with ratings of speech samples. The next study focused upon this question.

Brief descriptions (Williams et al. 1971a) of low and middle status black, white, and Mexican-American children were presented to respondents as stimuli; and white student teachers were asked to evaluate children whom they associated with these descriptions on scales relative to the two-factor model described earlier. A sample of one such description, this referring to a low status Mexican-American child, is as follows:

He is a Mexican-American boy who comes from a family of 10. His father is a gas station attendant. He lives in a lower class neighborhood.

In a preliminary evaluation session, respondents rated children associated with six such descriptions, representing low and middle status children from black, white, and Mexican-American groups in the central Texas area. Approximately one week after providing these ratings the group viewed and rated videotapes of children selected (by performance criteria) to represent the same six subgroups. Then at a period from three to five days after rating the videotapes, the respondents again evaluated stereotyped descriptions. This provided stereotyped descriptions rated at two different times and thus susceptible to comparison for consistency. The evaluations were a further basis for comparing the ratings of stereotype descriptions with ratings of samples of children's speech for representing the same categories. Figure 2 summarizes the results of the analysis of these data in terms of the two-factor model.

Note, first, in Figure 2 that for all three of the ethnic groups the stereotype evaluations obtained at two different times (m_1, m_2) were very consistent with one another. Note next that the stereotypes of the middle status children were always in the upper right-hand quadrant (indicating relatively high ratings on 'confidence-eagerness' and low ratings on 'ethnicity-nonstandardness') as against the lower status stereotypes appearing in the lower left quadrant, which reflecte

FIGURE 2.   Comparisons of stereotype and videotape ratings.

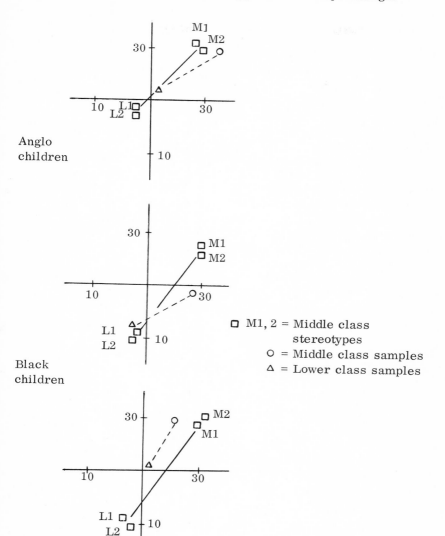

Anglo
children

Black
children

Mexican American
children

the opposite of the above ratings. Finally, it can be noted that for the most part, ratings of videotapes of the middle status and lower status children in each of the three ethnic groups tended in the direction of the stereotype ratings. There were exceptions to this; but such exceptions were usually only on one of the two dimensions. For example, on the ratings of the middle status black children, although the middle class videotape was rated as more 'ethnic-nonstandard' than was the stereotype, it was approximately the same as the stereotype in terms of confidence-eagerness.

The generalizations from this study were: (1) that one could readily obtain anticipated or stereotyped attitudes associated with a particular type of child, (2) that these would be consistent, (3) that they could be interpreted on the two-factor model, and (4) that they would show an interpretable relation with ratings of videotape samples.

A major problem in the study just described was that the verbal descriptions of the children used to elicit the stereotypes reflected directly on some of the scales relative to the two-factor model. In other words, the descriptions may have been sufficiently explicit so as to be more directly reflected in some of the scale ratings than they were a stimulus cue to have the individual respondent reflect his stereotype. Accordingly, in a further study (Williams, Whitehead, and Miller 1971a, 1972) it was found that ratings could be obtained simply by presenting a teacher with an ethnic label of a child and asking her to rate her experiences with, and anticipations of, children of that type. This time, the stimuli used to elicit stereotype ratings said nothing about status nor did they incorporate any adjectives which might directly influence the ratings. Figure 3 represents the stereotype evaluations of the labels 'anglo', [1] 'black', and 'Mexican-American' children as obtained from 125 white and 75 black teachers sampled from schools in central Texas.

At first it may be noted that these stereotypes are in somewhat different positions from those shown in Figure 2. This is anticipated because these stereotypes were not differentiated in their description by child status. Also some differences might be expected because these data came from groups of teachers practicing in the field, whereas the earlier data came from student teachers. In interpreting Figure 3, it can be noted that there is a general differentiation of the stereotypes of the three ethnic groups in the two-factor model, with the white children being located in the upper right quadrant, Mexican-Americans in the lower left, and black children tending toward the lower right. There is a greater differentiation between the white and black children's stereotypes in terms of 'ethnicity-nonstandardness' than in terms of 'confidence-eagerness'. The Mexican-American children's stereotypes were rated the least 'confident-eager' of all three groups, roughly similar to black children in terms of

FIGURE 3. Stereotype attitudes associated with 'anglo', 'black', and 'Mexican-American' children.

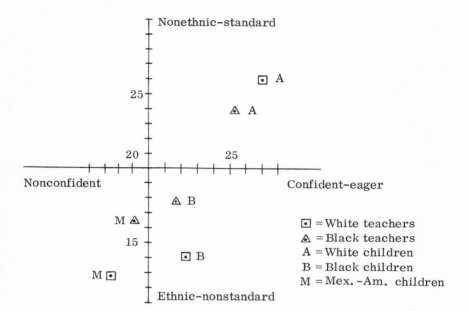

'ethnicity-nonstandardness' and markedly more 'ethnic-nonstandard' and less 'confident-eager' than the white children's stereotypes. It was evident, too, in this summary of stereotype ratings that the black and white teachers differed in their stereotypes. Black teachers tended to rate black children as less 'ethnic-nonstandard' than they were rated by white teachers. At the same time the black teachers rated white children as slightly more 'ethnic-nonstandard' and less 'confident-eager' than did white teachers. White teachers rated Mexican-American children as more 'ethnic-nonstandard' and slightly less 'confident-eager' than did black teachers.

By comparing the stereotype ratings with the ratings that the same groups of teachers gave of videotape samples of the speech of children from lower and middle status ethnic groups, it is possible to see how the stereotype related to different videotape ratings. Figure 4 is a summary of the low and middle status ratings of white children's videotapes by black and white teachers from central Texas schools. Note first that the videotape ratings all appear in the same quadrant as the stereotype ratings. More important is that the stereotype ratings have a tendency to stand between the middle and low status videotape ratings. For example, the geometric mean between the middle and the low status videotape ratings of anglo children by black teachers would almost perfectly define the location of the stereotype rating. The stereotype rating of white children by white teachers stands roughly between the two videotape ratings in terms of 'ethnicity-nonstandardness', but here the stereotype is rated as more 'confident-eager' than either of the videotapes.

The average ratings of the lower and middle status videotapes of black children are summarized in Figure 5. Here for both the ratings by black teachers and by white teachers the stereotyped rating falls almost at the mid point between the middle status and low status videotapes. In brief, the middle status tapes are rated more in the direction of 'nonethnic-sounding' and more 'confident-eager', as against the lower status tapes being rated the reverse of these from the stereotype. In this case, even more so than in the ratings of the white children, the videotapes of the different status groups tend to be differentiated away from the stereotype along a general diagonal direction that marks the patterns of differentiation in the model.

FIGURE 4. Ratings of white children's videotapes compared with stereotypes.

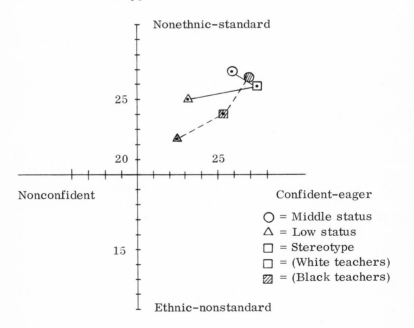

FIGURE 5. Ratings of black children's videotapes compared with stereotypes.

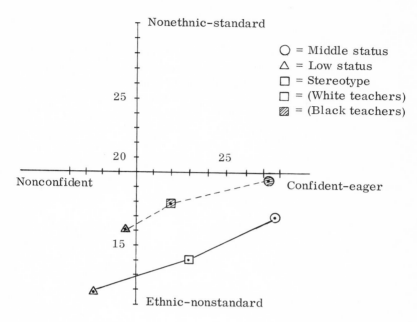

The videotape ratings of middle and lower status Mexican-American children and the stereotypes are summarized in Figure 6. Here there is no evidence of the stereotype standing between the middle status and lower status ratings of the children. In both cases of ratings by white teachers and black teachers the stereotypes are rated as less 'confident-eager' and more 'ethnic-nonstandard' than either of the tapes from the status groups. On the other hand, it can be noted that the middle and lower status tapes are differentiated from one another along the diagonal of the model. That is, the middle status tapes are rated as more 'confident-eager' and less 'ethnic-nonstandard' than the lower status opposites.

Some generalizations and speculations. In the stereotyping studies just described, it is evident that the stereotype judgments appear related to the judgments of speech samples. Although videotapes tend to show ratings that are biased in the same diagonal distribution as the stereotypes and even biased to the stereotypes themselves, the videotape ratings do not simply represent a person's report of the stereotype. Put another way, if a person's ratings of his speech stimuli were simply his stereotype or even extremely biased by his

FIGURE 6. Ratings of Mexican-American children's videotapes compared with stereotypes.

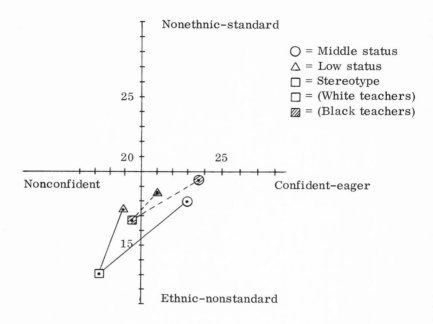

stereotype, we would expect to find the distribution of the videotape ratings on the two-factor model very close to those of the stereotype ratings. We find instead that the videotape ratings tend to be differentiated in a diagonal direction about the stereotypes. This is shown most clearly in the study just described, where the stereotype stimulus was simply a label of a child from a particular ethnic group, and the videotapes were chosen to represent status differentiations. Such status differentiations, with the exception of the Mexican-American children, [2] could almost be used to define or to predict the position of the stereotype. Or, by the same token, the stereotype could define, more or less, an anchor point about which videotapes are evaluated by the respondent.

In most of the considerations of the two-factor model prior to the stereotype research, it was assumed that persons provided attitudinal evaluations of children's audiotapes or videotapes by differentiating them relative to the neutral points on the model (or '20' in the preceding figures). That is, a child would be differentiated on 'ethnicity-nonstandardness' to the degree that the respondent would mark in cells away from the center (neutral) position on scales indexing that dimension, and would mark similarly for scales on 'confidence-eagerness'. The studies just discussed suggest that respondents may not differentiate the individual audiotape or videotape stimuli about the neutral point of the two-factor model, but instead may differentiate stimuli about a stereotype which is, more or less, an anchor point.

Of course, the present results do not unequivocally demonstrate that the stereotype is an anchor point; but they do offer quite suggestive evidence of it. The process of evaluation may be one where the stimulus may offer minimal cues which elicit a stereotype, then the stimulus is to various degrees differentiated by the respondent about the stereotype. This reasoning leads to a variety of implications. For one thing, it suggests that the teacher respondents do not evaluate children from different ethnic groups in a common way. Although it seems evident that the same two global dimensions of evaluation are used for the three ethnic groups of children, each child had a different 'starting point', so to speak, in how he was evaluated within the relative space of the two evaluative dimensions. Thus, for example, if a person's stereotype for black children tended to be biased in association with ethnic and nonstandard qualities and if the stereotype of the white child tended to be biased more toward the opposite extreme, it might be the case that the black child would have to sound more standard than the white child in order to obtain the same absolute rating. An alternative is that the respondent would have to free his or her ratings as much as possible from the stereotype bias that seems evident in the present studies.

Data from one further study (Williams, Whitehead, and Miller 1971b) show some evidence of how this bias may effect ratings. Figure 7 presents a plot of the average stereotype ratings by (white) student teachers of black, Mexican-American, and white children. It also presents the average ratings of three videotape presentations but where each had the same standard English audio track. The videotapes were side views of children whom could be seen speaking but whose utterances could not be lip read. Audio tracks of the standard English passage were dubbed onto the videotapes of the children from the three ethnic groups.[3] Note in Figure 7 that the same speech sample (the audio track) was rated quite differently depending upon which 'ethnic guise' it was presented with. Thus the black child with a standard English sound track was rated as more 'ethnic-nonstandard' than was the anglo child. The Mexican-American child is rated as markedly less 'confident-eager'. Of particular note, however, is that the biases in rating the standard English passage when paired with the two minority group children appear to be in the direction of the stereotype ratings of those two minority group children. The implication is that the visual image of the children on the tape served as an immediate cue of a type of child. This elicited a

FIGURE 7. Ratings of the same standard English audio samples with anglo, black, and Mexican-American video images.

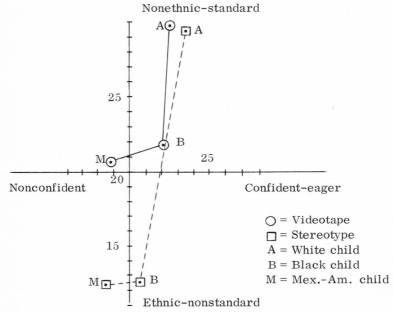

stereotype, and the presentation was judged relative to that stereotype. It is thought that this type of comparison represents the beginning of ways to test the degree to which ratings may be affected by manipulating the respondent's stereotypes. It is important to note, however, that this study only involved a relatively small group of student teachers and a limited number of stimuli. More important, some of the scales used in this research may apply equally well to the visual image as well as the audio track. Thus we can not assume that the respondent evaluates what is said as exactly distinct from what is seen. A further selection of scales that are more modality specific should aid in solving this problem in future studies.

At the outset of this paper it was said that my thesis was that persons have stereotyped sets of attitudes about dialects of speakers and that these attitudes play a role in how a person perceives another person's speech characteristics. Now stated more substantively, my thesis is that persons tend to employ stereotyped sets of attitudes as anchor points for their evaluation of whatever is presented to them as a sample of a person's speech. The description of this phenomenon in the present research is, of course, limited to the teacher and student populations which were sampled. My thesis is also limited at this point to the two-factor model of 'ethnicity-nonstandardness' and 'confidence-eagerness' which has been found in various groups of teachers. So, too, are the speech samples limited, mostly to standard English-speaking situations that could be classified as formal or semiformal. The extent to which this thesis of stereotyped attitudes affecting dialect perception would extend to other populations of evaluators, speakers, or speech situations, remains for further research. Fortunately, we appear to have the tools for that research.

NOTES

[1] The term for whites in central Texas.

[2] The exception of the Mexican-American children to this pattern between stereotypes and videotapes suggests some speculations. One is that the researchers' selection of the Mexican-American children for the videotapes was biased away from the stereotype--that is, they were more 'confident-eager' and nonethnic sounding than most respondents' stereotypes. Another speculation is that the stereotype of the Mexican-American child may be tied to the hesitancy of many of them to use English in formal situations and thus to say very little in teacher-pupil interactions; all of which might represent extremes in reticence and ethnic qualities to a white or black teacher.

[3] There were actually two standard English audio tracks used for each videotape; their average ratings are shown here. This was for research design requirements.

REFERENCES

Labov, W. 1966. The social stratification of English in New York City. Washington, D.C., Center for Applied Linguistics.
Shuy, R. 1969. Subjective judgments in sociolinguistic analysis. In: Linguistics and the teaching of standard English to speakers of other languages or dialects. Ed. by J. E. Alatis. Washington, D.C., Georgetown University.
Williams, F. 1970a. Language, attitude and social change. In: Language and poverty: perspectives on a theme. Ed. by F. Williams. Chicago, Markham.
_____. 1970b. Psychological correlates of speech characteristics: on sounding 'disadvantaged'. Journal of Speech and Hearing Research. 13.472-88.
_____, J. L. Whitehead, and L. M. Miller. 1971a. Attitudinal correlates of children's speech characteristics. USOE Research Report Project No. 0-0336.

128 / FREDERICK WILLIAMS

Williams, F., J. L. Whitehead, and L. M. Miller. 1971b. Ethnic
   stereotyping and judgments of children's speech. Speech Monographs. 38.166-70.
_____, J. L. Whitehead, and J. Traupmann. 1971. Teachers'
   evaluations of children's speech. Speech Teacher. 20.247-54.
_____, J. L. Whitehead, and L. M. Miller. 1972. Relations between
   language attitudes and teacher expectancy. American Educational
   Research Journal.
_____ and W. A. Shamo. 1972. Regional variations in teachers'
   attitudes toward children's language. Central States Speech
   Journal.

ATTITUDES TOWARD SPANISH AND QUECHUA IN BILINGUAL PERU[1]

WOLFGANG WÖLCK

State University of New York at Buffalo

1.0. The language situation. Peru is, like all the other countries in South and Central America, a multilingual nation. As in the other cases, its multilingualism is primarily the result of contact between native American (Indian) languages and a colonial (European) language, and, to a lesser extent, between different indigenous languages. The Peruvian situation is unique in that this country contains within its national boundaries the main portion of the largest surviving native language group in the Americas. Quechua, as this language of the pre-colonial Inca empire is now commonly called, is still spoken by approximately seven million people in the Andean republics, with the bulk of its speakers in the southern and central Peruvian Andes mountains. According to the Peruvian national census of 1961, 40% of its total population of close to twelve million people speak Quechua as their first language. Of the other indigenous languages, only Aymara, the closest relative to Quechua, occupies by itself a clearly recognized slot, although with little more than 200,000 speakers it tends to be quantitatively overshadowed by Quechua. The multitude of languages spoken on the eastern slopes of the Andes and in the jungle area along the tributaries of the Amazon account for less than 100,000 people by the most generous assessment, the largest single component being the Campa, members of the Arawak family.[2] Among the Campa and Aymara, we find the largest number of bilinguals in indigenous languages, with Quechua as their second language. Moreover, trilingualism is quite frequent among these people through the addition

129

of Spanish, the country's national language, to their reperotire. By far the most frequent point of contact, however, is clearly that between Spanish and Quechua: 20% of the total population above five years of age is said to be bilingual in Quechua and Spanish. This leaves about half the Quechua-speaking population monolingual and outside the socio-political life of that sector of Peru which would like to be considered representative of the role of this country in today's world.

The proportions become more extreme when we look at the Andean departments of Peru. There, as, e.g. in the Department of Ayacucho, Quechua is the mother tongue of 95%, Spanish of only 5%, of the population. Here, then, the proportion of bilinguals is somewhat higher than the national average, with a disproportion of two to one of men against women. The number of bilinguals is a little larger than, or equal to, the number of literates--with the same disproportion between males and females. In urban areas the percentages of bilinguals and literates are three times higher than in rural areas, where the proportion of literate males versus females often drops to three to one.

1.2. The Peruvian survey ('El Proyecto BQC'). Bilingualism--literacy--education--integration--is considered to be the safest route that promises to lead these 'marginated'[3] very sizable populations into bearable standards of living and that might even make them contribute to the country's GNP. Although Quechua had never been fully recognized or officialized on equal grounds with Spanish, it had always played some, however minor, role on the Peruvian educational scene. Recent governments and ministers of education have become increasingly more favorable toward 'bilingual education', i.e. using the native language of the Indian population as at least a means, if not a subject, of instruction to smooth the road toward literacy and further education. One such program started in 1964 under the auspices of the Plan for Linguistic Development of the Peruvian National University of San Marcos.[4] The results, though respectable, have been somewhat more modest than expected. In an effort to get to the roots of the problem, I was invited in early 1969 to begin a sociolinguistic survey of Quechua-Spanish bilingualism in Peru. The methodology of this project has been described in detail elsewhere.[5] As of this date, we have completed about 200 full-scale interviews in three locations, one a remote village in the Department of Ayacucho, another a district in the departmental capital of Ayacucho, and the most recent in the 'barriadas' of Lima, where we interviewed in-migrants from the first two locations. Most of the interviews were tape recorded and then transferred, i.e. abstrated, onto language

background questionnaires. The responses are currently being tabulated and evaluated.

2.0. The attitude test. During the initial phase of the Project
which began in the summer of 1969, while we were still largely involved in preparatory work for the general plan of the survey, we
decided to devise a brief pretest or pilot study of language attitudes
to be administered in our first two work sites. Besides developing
and testing the instrument as such, one small immediate objective
was the investigation of the validity of the two most current popular
attitudes towards the language problem, which we shall call the
'hispanicist' and 'indigenist' attitudes, respectively. Extreme
followers of the first position favor the speediest hispanicization of
the non-Spanish speaking population over the retention of their own
language, while the proponents of the latter doctrine tend to deny
the usefulness or necessity of a knowledge of Spanish in their effort
to preserve the native language and culture. [6]
The format we chose was that of a scaled instrument based on controlled language stimuli. [7] While we were quite aware of the separate
tasks of preparing the stimuli and developing the rating scales, the
importance of defining and selecting the evaluative terms for use in
the instrument as a distinct job has become increasingly obvious
since we began this study. [8]

2.1. The selection of the stimulus. To simulate as closely as
possible the characteristics of conversational speech, we decided to
use samples of connected free speech rather than isolated utterances
as in the case of the Larsens' project. Carolyn and Vernon Larsen,
of Social Science Research Associates in Chicago, were kind enough
to let me see the materials they used in their study of reactions to
black and white speech in Chicago. [9] Their study and its methodology
clearly inspired this one. However, if isolated words are chosen as
samples or stimuli, it is obviously only a very small subset of the
phonological representations which can be at variance and will,
therefore, be able to influence the judgment of the hearer. Yet it
is most reasonable to assume that all levels of linguistic expression
will be utilized by a hearer as diagnostic of the speaker's status,
notably morphosyntactic features, lexical selection, ease of expression, articulatory distinctness, speed of delivery, and so on. The
hearer should have access to all these potential variables when asked
to judge another person's speech. Using connected speech, on the
other hand, presents many problems that would not arise with isolated
word stimuli. Some of the extra-linguistic variables in the message
that might influence a rater's judgment are very difficult to control.
The individual voice timbre can clearly not be neutralized. Others--

like contextual indicators of the speaker's status--can and must be eliminated from the passages used. Another important decision concerns the 'content' of the passages used for testing. Certain topics which might evoke different emotional reactions among different respondents and, therefore, influence their rating have to be avoided.

In addition, then, to insisting on as free as possible and continuous speech for our stimulus, we set up the following criteria for the choice of test passages. Some would apply to all stimuli used in attitude testing. Some, like the last, are specific to situations where cultural differences parallel linguistic ones.

(1) They should all have approximately the same content.

(2) The topic should be one of current validity, familiar to all speakers of the samples, and--possibly--the jury, to ensure ease and fluency in discussing it.

(3) The topic should have minimal emotional appeal. For example, choosing the description of a football (i.e. soccer) match in Latin America, even though it would satisfy criteria (1) and (2), might distract the rater from an evaluation of the speech sample to critical appraisal of the speaker's accuracy in reporting or interpreting the game. (Countries have been known to go to war over such matters.)

(4) The topic should be indigenous to both language communities, the Spanish and the Quechua-speaking group, and should be describable by a maximally independent vocabulary in both languages.

The topic which we eventually chose was bullfighting. Though it did not fulfill each separate criterion ideally, it combined a high degree of satisfaction over all of them.

Each speaker was asked to relate the events of a country bullfight which, by the way, is quite different from a Spanish-style bullfight as practiced in the Lima bullring. Country bullfights are an integral part of the independence-day celebration and are a free-for-all, fun-for-all event where anyone who has drunk himself into sufficient courage will confront the bull. Style and technique matter little, quite unlike the famous Spanish 'corrida'.

The bilingual test speakers were asked to describe the event in both Spanish and Quechua. We added a neutral specimen consisting of counting from 1 to 10, or 11 to 20, recorded for each speaker. Due to the rater fixed sequence of the events in the ceremony, it could be expected that the accounts would vary little in their content and its order. The recordings indeed showed many parallelisms, even though the informants had not received any special instructions beyond some general suggestions as to what we wanted them to talk about.

Besides the bullfighting stories, we recorded from each informant an account of a different event well-known in the area, a so-called 'pachamanca', which is a kind of picnic or cook-out with many libations, enjoyed among friends and family on special occasions. In terms of comparability or likeness of content, however, the 'corrida' was a much better topic.

The original recorded samples were left largely unedited. The only information that was cut out or masked over with played-in background noise concerned instances of possible explicit or implicit indicators of status. We also reduced extra-long pauses, although this may be objected to on the grounds that ease of expression is a possible index of status. All test samples were kept to approximately two and one-half minutes in length. If this required cuts, they were made at the beginning and/or the end of the original recording, where they coincided with paragraph or context boundaries. Within the sample no cuts were made unless it was to eliminate extralinguistic personal identifiers.

2.2. The informants. The speakers who produced the stimuli for the tests described here were chosen from two social and two linguistic groups. We used two Quechua-Spanish bilinguals of different social status, one of whom might be called a member of the middle class. He has a college education and comes from a moderately wealthy family. His parents are also bilingual. The other works as a driver and did not finish secondary school. His parents, who farm a small lot outside the departmental capital, know hardly any Spanish. He would be a member of the lower or lower middle class. The third speaker in this group was monolingual in Spanish and had spent only a few years in the area, working in the town's only large hotel as an accountant. He would also qualify for middle class membership. These three speakers were all males in their mid-twenties; two were interviewed by the same bilingual member of our team in Quechua, while I did the interviewing in Spanish. By situational criteria, the styles of the connected speech samples could be labeled informal, though not quite colloquial, rather like Joos's consultative style.[10] In age, average voice pitch, and volume, the speakers were very similar.

The total 'independent' controlled 'variables'--at least the ones we thought we controlled--in our stimuli were, then:

(1) the social class of the speaker,
(2) the language capacity of the speaker, i.e. whether he was monolingual or bilingual,
(3) the language used in the stimulus,
(4) the topic discussed in the stimulus passage.

2.3. The arrangement of the passages for testing. Up till now, we have worked with three different combinations of test passages. All our test tapes contain a total of six samples, each about two and one-half minutes long.

On the first test tape we had only two speakers, the higher- and the lower-class bilingual. We used passages in Spanish and Quechua from both, dealing with two different topics. In detail: In the first sample, the middle-class speaker talks about a picnic in Spanish; in the second, the lower-class speaker relates part of a bullfight in Quechua; in the third, the higher-class speaker does the same; in the fourth, the lower-class speaker describes the bullfight in Spanish; the fifth has the higher-class speaker depicting a bullfight in Spanish; the sixth and last is another two and one-half minute portion taken from the lower-class speaker's account of the bullfight in Quechua. It is distinct from the earlier, second passage on the tape, though only minimally, as the same speaker is talking about the same topic in the same language.

2.3.1. Variation of topic and consistency check. The rationale behind the topic variation was to see whether and how it would affect the response. The results, after tabulation and evaluation of the responses, showed that it did not.

Samples 2 and 6 were kept minimally distinct in content to avoid possible recognition of the speaker's identity by the audience. The purpose of introducing two near-identical samples was to test the jury's consistency in rating. This turned out to be an unnecessary precaution. No juror seemed to be aware that any one speaker was being used more than once. Even those who seemed to have noticed that some speaker had appeared more than once could not be specific about their hunches. On the basis of these results, we changed the arrangement on our second test tape and substituted an identical re-play of the second sample--the lower-class speaker's bullfight story in Quechua--for the last sample as a better instrument for a consistency or reliability measure. In our latest re-arrangement of the test tape, we also discarded passage one, the only one left with a topic other than bullfighting, and put a recording of the middle-class monolingual's Spanish account of the bullfight in its place. On this test tape, then, the topic was invariant, and we had samples from three speakers--one from the middle-class monolingual in Spanish, and one each in Spanish and in Quechua from both the middle-class and the lower-class bilingual, with a repetition of the lower-class Quechua sample.

2.4. The rating scales. In devising a rating scale, we adopted the semantic differential technique as originally developed by Osgood and associates for cognitive studies,[11] together with an occupational suitability scale.

2.4.1. Semantic differential. In trying to establish the validity of a certain pair of polar terms for diagnostic purposes, we relied mostly on common, locally frequent concepts of evaluation and designation. Through observation and testing of associations, we first singled out a large number of apparently useful epithets. Reasons for later elimination of some were mostly of two kinds: One was that a common evaluative term turned out to vary too much in associations or that it had regionally distinct connotations, as was the case with the well-known Latin(-American) simpático, which to our surprise seems to refer exclusively to external attractiveness in the Peruvian Andes. Another reason was the impossibility of finding a parametrical antonym for a good term to make up a useful pair, as in the case of forastero for a non-local person or indio, where no good contrast exists. Negating the positive is no really good solution, although we sometimes used this way out, as in 'responsable--irresponsable', which is still better than 'amable--no-amable', while negation of adjectives and nouns in Spanish in this manner might even be rejected for reasons of grammaticality. We eventually decided upon the fifteen pairs of adjectives and nouns that can be found in the Appendix. An English translation of the terms is provided there.

The terms used in the scales were not chosen, or classified, by any other criteria like 'power versus solidarity',[12] 'cognitive versus affective', or any other such classificatory or general semantic notions.

Most of the concepts and attributes on the list will be reasonably clear. The English glosses, though they do not evoke associations completely identical to the Spanish, may help a little. One pair, though, definitely needs further comment. This is the distinction cholo--decente. Although its popular connotation is clearly negative, the anthropologist's neutral scientific use of the term cholo might help illustrate its meaning. The social anthropologist distinguishes between Indians, Cholos, and Mestizos by cultural integration and nativistic loyalty (Linton's term).[13] Thus cholo refers to a person who has left the Indian culture and has not yet been integrated into the Western, Spanish-speaking Mestizo culture. Popular usage collapses Indian and Cholo under the latter term, abstracting only the negative features in its employment. The term is emotionally loaded. Cholo, no estas en la sierra is the worst rapping a Limeño will give to another who steps out of line, as, for example, disturbing traffic through bad driving, or the like. Decentre, on the other hand, is the opposite of cholo in social status connotation. It implies being educated, respected, having adequate knowledge of Spanish.

The introduction of language competence scales (pairs B and K) was intended to serve as a preliminary subjective assessment of degrees of bilingualism.

2.4.2. The occupational suitability scale. Again, all the occupations selected for inclusion are well known to the juries which judged our samples. In deciding about distinctiveness, consistency of rating and ranking, we first presented a random list of over twenty occupations for hierarchical ranking to a large number of subjects (see Appendix). We selected those with a sufficiently small range of fluctuation. Certain seemingly clear cases turned out to be very ambiguous, as, for instance, hacendado, which to the rural poor would only mean a big landowner, while higher-class members would understand it as meaning any farmer, big or small. Chacarero, on the other hand--which, incidentally, is a Quechua loanword--refers usually to a small subsistence farmer.

A curious marginal result of this ranking poll was that female rankers would put jobs that are more indicative of material wealth first, before those involving intellectual prestige or academic training; the males would rank the other way around.

The hierarchical ascending scale of twelve occupations (see Appendix) was what we ended up with for the time being. It should be read top to bottom in left to right column sequence.

2.5.1. Administration of the test. The testing pad consisted of six identical rating sheets, one for each of the six test stimuli on the tape; an instruction sheet on top as introduction; and a personal data sheet at the end. Plus and minus sides of the pairs were randomly scrambled to avoid the possible suggestion of directionality to the respondent (see Appendix). We chose a six-interval scale, forcing the respondents to make a choice or leave a line blank. Odd-number interval scales leave the option of undecidedness, which may be different from the rater's decision not to respond to a certain pair at all. During the administration of the test, each stimulus was played to the responding audience or jury only once, sufficient time allowed for checking on the rating sheet, and then on to the next stimulus.

2.5.2. The respondents. Our raters, or jurors, were final-grade primary school boys, high school students, university students, and a small group of teachers--all male, with the exception of a few women teachers.

2.5.3. Tabulation of responses. The very first step in processing consisted of transferring the ratings of each stimulus separately onto a table with the pairs and occupations listed horizontally, the respondents vertically, and ratings being indicated by the number checked on each scale, i. e. a value between 0 and 5.

The next job was calculating the consistency of ratings for each respondent by comparing his responses to the two identical stimuli, number 2 and number 6. For our present purposes, we considered anyone with a higher average than 1.0 difference between the responses to the two identical passages as potentially unreliable for the other ratings. From the tables of individual ratings per stimulus, averages can be computed for any defined set of respondents. Such an average rating of a certain stimulus can then be plotted for each pair on an evaluation sheet where all contrasts are listed in the same direction, i. e. negatives on the left, positives on the right. The Appendix includes such 'profiles', shown as contrasting pairs on two scoring sheets.

3.0. Some test results. Before going into more detail, we would like to mention a general result which emerged immediately after the first tabulations, even though it may not be theoretically surprising. The terms on our scales fell neatly into two groups by differential reactions to the two sets. One set included the terms with some sort of institutional reference, like 'low-class--high class', 'educated--uneducated', 'urban--rural', while pairs with more emotive or associative value like 'ugly--pretty', 'weak--strong', 'kind--unkind', made up the other set. This post factum reinstatement of Osgood's classification (cognitive-affective) may be of some importance.

3.1. Language and social status. The profiles in the Appendix are plotted from the reactions to two Spanish stimuli by a class of male university students in their early twenties. The double line there shows their rating of the lower-class speaker's Spanish; the single line is for the middle-class speaker. The result that is typical of all the audiences we have worked with is that the higher-class speaker is given a clearly superior rating in the majority of cases, notably in those with a clear referent, like 'campo--ciudad' (rural--urban), 'empleado--jefe' (worker--boss), low-class--high-class, educated--uneducated, or on the occupational scale. The tendency for the lower-class speaker to come out relatively better on the affective judgment is already evident here, in the ranking of his Spanish performance. It comes out clearly in such pairs as 'amable--no amable', 'responsable--irresponsable'.

3.2. Quechua versus Spanish. Probably the most interesting result is the affective loyalty to Quechua which becomes evident when we compare the profiles of the responses to the same speaker's

performances in Quechua and in Spanish (see Appendix). In this case
the double line denotes Spanish, the single one Quechua. His Spanish
always receives a higher ranking on the referential scale, i. e.
higher-class, urban, more educated, than his Quechua. The rating
by the affective criteria, however, shows a clear preference for
Quechua. When speaking Quechua, he is rated stronger, more sin-
cere, less arrogant, more ambitious, smarter, than when he speaks
Spanish.

The results of the test indicate that, by identifiable social status
criteria, Quechua is stigmatized but that there is, nevertheless, a
great deal of native loyalty shown to the language, borne out on the
affective scales.

3.3. Language competence. Another important bit of evidence,
borne out by the reaction of all respondents alike, concerns the concept of linguistic competence measured by the pairs referring to
knowledge of Quechua and Spanish, respectively (pairs B and K).
First--and this might have been predicted--the lower-class speaker's
Spanish was rated as inferior to the higher-class informant's, but--
and this is curious--his Quechua was also rated poorer than the
higher-status speaker's. The seemingly strange request for the
knowledge of Quechua to be rated even if Spanish was spoken, and
vice versa, gave most interesting though perhaps not entirely surprising results: When the lower-class speaker was using Spanish,
he received an equal or higher ranking on knowledge of Quechua than
when he spoke Quechua. His Quechua, on the other hand, was rated
only minimally lower than his Spanish on the 'knowledge-of-Spanish'
criterion. The higher-class speaker, conversely, received a low
rating on Quechua when he spoke Spanish, and a similarly low rating
on Spanish when he spoke Quechua.

When speaking Spanish, Speaker 1 (Spanish-Quechua bilingual)
and Speaker 3 (Spanish monolingual) received equally low ratings on
the knowledge-of-Quechua scale, Speaker 2 (low-class bilingual) a
much higher rating than either 1 or 3. The lower-class bilingual's
Quechua seems to have little societal value in the response of hearers.
While it makes his Spanish worse, it does not help his Quechua performance any. That is, at least, the superficial impression. The
linguist, however, will see in these results an interesting indication
of grammatical integration: The grammar of the lower-class bilingual is obviously simpler in terms of identifying and collapsing
more rules of the two systems into one, besides substituting more
lexical items in both directions (or only in one), while the better
educated bilingual has a much less fused grammar. The established
concept and interpretation of 'interference'[14] does not seem to fit
this bilingual situation, but may have to be complemented and, in

this instance, replaced by the process which, for the time being, we have called 'fusion'. [15]

3.4. Differences between groups of raters.

3.4.1. Degree of bilingualism. The stablest bilinguals showed the least difference between ratings of Spanish and Quechua stimuli on the 'referential' scales. There appears to be an inverse proportion between the degree of bilingualism and the status differentiation between the two languages. Language dominance, whether Quechua or Spanish happens to be the dominant language, seems to have little effect on this principle. If plotted in a diagram, the curve showing the proportion between the degree of bilingualism and the evaluative status distinction between the two languages would approach the following form:

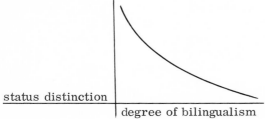

status distinction

degree of bilingualism

On the 'affective' scale, there is a gradual decrease in the amount of positive evaluation of Quechua the more heavily Spanish-dominant the bilinguals are:

(1) The Quechua-dominant bilinguals rate Quechua as less lazy or more industrious, smarter, stronger, more honest, less arrogant, more pleasant or kinder, nicer ('amable'), i.e. more positively on practically all the affective scales.

(2) The stable or matched bilinguals ('ambilinguals') show distinct positive evaluation for Quechua only on the strength, amiability, and smartness scales.

(3) The Spanish-dominant group shows a differential rating that is positive for Quechua only on the strength and attractiveness ('bonito') scales. On most of the other affective markers the two languages come very close; on the 'lazy-ambitious' scale there is even a change-over in favor of Spanish. Quechua seems to be rated here only as an aboriginal culture with its rather stereotyped epithets of being 'earthy' and 'quaint'.

3.4.2. Quechua speakers versus non-Quechua speakers. In only one jury, the one composed of university students, were we able to separate the Quechua speakers' from the non-Quechua speakers' reactions. In general, the results of this comparison conformed pretty much to the tendencies already observed as accompanying an increase in the dominance of the Spanish language, of which Spanish monolingualism may here be considered the end point.

One prominent difference, however, exists in the accuracy of the evaluation of linguistic competence of the bilingual speakers. The Quechua-Spanish bilinguals among our respondents showed a high and accurate degree of sensitivity to bilingual interference with regard to both languages, the monolinguals much less so.[16] The bilinguals were also much more sensitive to class dialects or styles within Quechua. They ranked the higher-class speaker clearly into the 'decente' range, even when he spoke Quechua, while for the monolinguals he was simply a 'cholo'.

To the bilinguals, the higher-class speaker is suspect, even when he speaks Quechua. He is less amiable ('amable') than the lower-class speaker, whereas the monolinguals rate the opposite way; the same is true for the arrogance scale.

NOTES

[1] An earlier report on this study was delivered at the 1970 meeting of the International Linguistics Association. The research reported in this paper was supported by a Latin American Studies grant from the Ford Foundation, an Indiana University Summer Faculty Fellowship, and by funds from the 'Plan de Fomento Lingüístico' of the Universidad Nacional Mayor de San Marcos in Lima, Peru. I am grateful to the current director of the Plan de Fomento Lingüístico, Dr. Inés Pozzi-Escot, and to its former director, Dr. Alberto Escobar, for their cooperation and encouragement. Any credit for this work I have to share with my Peruvian and North American research associates.

[2] These and later figures are based on the reports of the Sexto Censo Nacional de Población de 1961, Lima: Instituto Nacional de Planificación, Dirección Nacional de Estadística y Censos, 1965-1970; in particular on the following volumes: III: Idioma, alfabetismo, asistencia escolar, nivel de educación. Centros poblados I: Amazonas Ancash, Apurimac, Arequipa, Ayacucho, and on the special volume for the Department of Ayacucho (in preparation; the tables were made available to us). Figures for 'jungle' languages are from C. F. and F. M. Voegelin: Languages of the World: Native America, Anthropological Linguistics, vol. 6, no. 6 (1964) and vol. 7, no. 7 (1965) and from information received from the staff of the Summer Institute of Linguistics in Peru. For location and classification see also

Čestmír Loukotka, Classification of South American indian languages, Los Angeles, University of California, 1968.

[3]A gloss attempting to capture the flavor of the official Peruvian euphemism commonly applied to these people, 'marginado', pushed to the margin, i.e. left out.

[4]Descriptions of this program are Inés Pozzi-Escot: La Educación rural en el Peru: El problema de los quechua-hablantes, Actas del Primer Seminario de Investigación y Ensenanza de la Lingüística, Concepción 1971:99-104, and her paper, La situacion lingüística en el Peru y su repercusión en la enseñanza del castellano, read at the First International Workshop in Andean Linguistics in Buffalo, New York, August 1971. Another program of bilingual education is being undertaken by members of the Summer Institute of Linguistics. Cf. Donald Burns, Bilingual education in the Andes of Peru. In: Language problems of developing nations. Ed. by J. A. Fishman, C. A. Ferguson, and J. Das Gupta. New York, John Wiley, 1968:403-13, and his Cinco anos de educacion bilingue en los Andes del Perú, report presented to the First International Workshop in Andean Linguistics, Buffalo 1971.

[5]See W. Wölck, El Proyecto BQC: Metodología de una encuesta sociolingüística sobre el bilingüismo Quechua-Castellano. In: Lingüística e indigenismo moderno de América. Ed. by G. J. Parker, A. G. Lozano, and R. Ravines. Estudios presentados al XXXIX Congreso Internacional de Americanistas, Lima (in press); and Teoría y práctica de la encuesta sociolingüística, in Proceedings of the 6th Symposium of the Interamerican Program for Linguistics and Language Teaching, San Juan (Puerto Rico) 1971.

[6]Cf. the debates in the proceedings of the Mesa redonda sobre el monolinguismo Quechua y Aymara y la educación en el Perú. Documentos Regionales de la Etnohistoria Andina 2. Lima, Casa de la Cultura, 1966.

[7]For a critical summary and bibliography of some of the practices in attitude testing, see Rebecca Agheyisi and Joshua A. Fishman: Language attitude studies: a brief survey of methodological approaches, Anthropological Linguistics. 12(5).137-57 (1970).

[8]See W. Wölck, Language as a basis for social attitudes, paper presented during the Sociolinguistics Forum of the 1971 Linguistic Institute.

[9]Vernon S. and Carolyn H. Larsen, Reactions to pronunciations, part of: Language barriers to communication. Chicago Sociolinguistics Project. (mimeographed) (1967).

[10]Cf. Martin Joos, The isolation of styles. In: Monograph Series on Languages and Linguistics No. 12 (10th Annual Round Table). Washington, D. C., Georgetown University Press, 1959, pp. 107ff.,

and The five clocks, Bloomington, Indiana, Research Center for
Anthropology, Folklore, and Linguistics, Publication 22, 1962.
    [11]Charles E. Osgood, G. J. Suci, and P. H. Tannenbaum, The
measurement of meaning. Urbana, University of Illinois Press,
1957.
    [12]As used by Joan Rubin, Bilingual use in Paraguay. In: Read-
ings in the sociology of language. Ed. by J. A. Fishman. The Hague
Mouton, 1968:512ff.
    [13]Ralph Linton, Nativistic movements, American Anthropologist.
45.230-40 (1943).
    [14]As defined in Uriel Weinreich, Languages in contact. The Hague
Mouton, 3rd pr. 1964.
    [15]In W. Wölck, Interference or fusion? A new look at the bi-
lingual's grammar. To be presented at the 11th International Linguistics Congress.
    [16]This parallels and again confirms Labov's observation of the
high sensitivity on the part of the users of certain stigmatized forms
to the occurrence of such forms in others, bearing out their 'linguistic insecurity'. Cf. William Labov, The social stratification of
English in New York City. Washington, D. C., Center for Applied
Linguistics, 1966, chaps, XI and XII.

APPENDIX

I. Scoring pad

    Desearíamos saber lo que Usted piensa acerca del habla (conver-
sación) o de las personal que hablan, luego de escucharlas a través
de cintas grabadas. No interesa la historia, sólo el habla y la
persona que habla.

    Instruciones. A. Damos una lista de pares de palabras con-
trarias con seis espacios entre ellas. Usted puede marcar su
opinión con un aspa (X) en el espacio que mejor corresponda a la
realidad.
    Suponiendo que el par de palabras sea 'agradable--desagradable'
luego de escuchar la cinta grabada si le parece: Muy agradable
puede marcar así:
    Agradable __X:___:___:___:___ Desagradable
Si le parece más o menos agradable puede marcar así:
    Agradable ___: X:___:___:___:___ Desagradable
Si le pareco poco agradable puede marcar así:
    Agradable ___:___: X :___:___:___ Desagradable

Si le parece muy desagradable puede marcar así:
Agradable ___:___:___:___:___: X Desagradable
Si le parece más o menos desagradable puede marcar así:
Agradable ___:___:___:___: X :___ Desagradable
Si le parec poco desagradable puede marcar así:
Agradable ___:___:___: X :___:___ Desagradable

Advertencias.
(1) Sólo debe haber un aspa entre dos pares de palabras.
(2) Sólo una vez se va a escuchar la cinta grabada.
(3) Hay una hoja para cada ejemplo de habla en la cinta grabada.

Les agradecemos su atención y colaboración y les pedimos que en la última hoja dé su nombre y otros datos que necesitamos.

Ejemplo número ___*

A.

feo	__:__:__:__:__:__	bonito
sabe quechua	__:__:__:__:__:__	no sabe quechua
empleado	__:__:__:__:__:__	jefe
fuerte	__:__:__:__:__:__	débil
ciudad	__:__:__:__:__:__	campo
mentriroso	__:__:__:__:__:__	sincero
clase alta	__:__:__:__:__:__	clase baja
amable	__:__:__:__:__:__	no amable
humilde	__:__:__:__:__:__	prepotente
sabe castellano	__:__:__:__:__:__	no sabe castellano
ambicioso	__:__:__:__:__:__	flojo
cholo	__:__:__:__:__:__	decente
sabido	__:__:__:__:__:__	tonto
irresponsable	__:__:__:__:__:__	responsable
ignorante	__:__:__:__:__:__	educado

B. Ocupación

_____ peón	_____ empleado
_____ obrero	_____ negociante
_____ chacarero	_____ maestro
_____ artesano	_____ sanitario
_____ chofer	_____ abogado
_____ albañil	_____ médico

*Identico para ejemplos nos. 2-6.

| Nombre | Apellido Paterno | Apellido Materno |

Edad_____ Sexo_____

Centro de enseñanza_____
Año_____ Grado de Instrucción_____
Profesor_____
Dirección_____
Lugar de Nacimiento_____
¿Sabe Ud. Quechua? Sí_____ No _____
Ocupación del padre_____
Viajes realizados (A dónde? ¿Por cuánto tiempo?)_____

Fecha_____

    II. Ranking list of occupations

1. médico	2. aboqado	3. maestro
4. fabricante	5. empleado	6. sanitario
7. chofer	8. albañil	9. hacendado
10. artesano	11. obrero	12. negociante
13. mozo	14. peón	15. chacarero

III. Attitude profiles (Univ. Nac. San Cristobal de Huamarga, Ayacucho, Jury)

Language: Spanish
Speaker I: Middle class; Speaker II: Lower middle class

A.

	0 1 2 3 4 5		
feo		bonito	A
no sabe quechua		sabe quechua	B
empleado		jefe	C
debil		fuerte	D
campo		ciudad	E
mentiroso		sincero	F
clase baja		clase alta	G
no amable		amable	H
prepotente		humide	J
no sabe castellano		sabe castellano	K
flojo		ambicioso	L
cholo		decente	M
tonto		sabido	N
irresponsable		responsable	O
ignorante		educado	P

B. Ocupacion

_____ peon	_____ empleado
_____ obrero	_____ negociante
_____ chacarero	I=○ maestro
II=◉ artesano	_____ sanitario
_____ chofer	_____ abogado
_____ albañil	_____ medico

Jury: Univ. students (UNSCH)
Stimuli: Quechua (—) and Spanish (=) by lower middle class speaker

A.   0   1   2   3   4   5

                        C   Q

feo	bonito	A
no sabe quechua	sabe quechua	B
empleado	jefe	C
debil	fuerte	D
campo	ciudad	E
mentiroso	sincero	F
clase baja	clase alta	G
no amable	amable	H
prepotente	humilde	J
no sabe casteliano	sabe castelliano	K
flojo	ambicioso	L
cholo	decente	M
tonto	sabido	N
irresponsable	responsable	O
ignorante	educado	P

Q C

B. Ocupacion

	peon		empleado
	obrero		negociante
Q=	chacarero		maestro
C=	artesano		sanitario
	chofer		abogado
	albañil		medico

A.

ugly	pretty	A
does not know Quechua	knows Quechua	B
employee	boss	C
weak	strong	D
country	city	E
dishonest	honest	F
lower class	higher class	G
unpleasant	pleasant	H
arrogant	unassuming	J
does not know Spanish	knows Spanish	K
lazy	ambitious	L
'cholo'	'decent folk'	M
dumb	smart	N
irresponsible	responsible	O
uneducated	educated	P

B.

peon	employee
workman	merchant
peasant	health officer
artesan	teacher
driver	lawyer
brick mason	doctor

OBJECTIVE AND SUBJECTIVE PARAMETERS OF LANGUAGE ASSIMILATION AMONG SECOND-GENERATION PUERTO RICANS IN EAST HARLEM

WALT WOLFRAM

Federal City College and Center for Applied Linguistics

> The Negroes were in New York first and had a head start, but now the Puerto Ricans are copying them. They are borrowing the Negroes' gang structure. Also their jive talk and bop language (Rand 1958:130).

Although there are a number of ways in which the sociolinguistic situation surrounding the second generation Puerto Rican in East Harlem parallels that of other immigrant groups, there are also many ways in which this sociolinguistic situation is unique. As part of a major immigrant group in New York City, the Puerto Rican child is born into a relatively homogeneous adult Hispanic community. Typically, his parents have sought out social relations with other Puerto Rican immigrants with whom they can continue Puerto Rican cultural and linguistic traditions. As a young child, the second-generation Puerto Rican is usually raised within the context of this community. His first language is Spanish, and he initially adopts the traditional Puerto Rican culture of his parents. The child, of course, has very little to say in this matter.

As he reaches adolescence, however, he establishes his own peers, and at this point more alternatives open up. He can obviously choose to continue his association with Puerto Rican peers with backgrounds quite similar to his own. If this alternative is chosen, he may remain a fairly integral part of the community, revealing many of the

148

linguistic and cultural traits which have been described for other homogeneous immigrant groups. But there are also other options which may arise due to certain physical and social conditions found in the context of East Harlem. It is a well-known fact that East Harlem is surrounded by the black community in the broader context of Harlem. Although there are obviously many differences between the lower-class black and Puerto Rican cultures, there is an affinity which may unite the groups because of the ethnic and social discrimination found in American society (this is particularly true of darker-skinned Puerto Ricans, who have less options in mainstream American culture than their lighter-skinned counterparts). Similar societal roles for Puerto Rican and black communities have been noted in a number of studies of Puerto Rican immigrants. For example, Mills et al. (1950:133) note:

> . . . he [i.e. the Puerto Rican] must 'become like' the Negro in the metropolitan community. The world in which he is to function inconspicuously is the Negro world . . . He finds that he can hold only certain jobs, mix socially only with certain people. Almost always he must live in the Harlem ghetto, or in certain Negro sections of the Bronx.

The similarity in social position, the physical proximity of the groups, and the inevitable social contact that must take place in neighborhood facilities (e.g. schools, recreational centers, etc.) provide an ideal situation for the study of language contact.

Sample. In an attempt to describe the sociolinguistic situation that exists among second-generation Puerto Ricans we have recently completed a study of forty-four informants, twenty-nine Puerto Rican and fifteen black informants. Parents of the Puerto Rican informants were born in Puerto Rico and migrated to the United States. The children, however, were born and raised in New York City.

According to most of the current indices for objectively measuring socioeconomic class, the informants would be classified as children of 'working' or lower-working class parents. The occupational roles of the heads of households are mainly restricted to operatives, service workers, and laborers. Although we have not made evaluations of all the individual residences of the informants, a survey of the general neighborhoods and observation of a sample of the projects and tenements in which the informants live indicates that they are quite typical of working or lower-working class residences in Harlem. Many of the residences would clearly be classified as slum dwellings.

The school records of the informants further indicate that, for the most part, their educational achievement is far below the expected norms for their age level. This was true of their reading levels in particular, a fact which was well confirmed by a small reading passage which was given as a part of the interview. Several of the informants would have to be considered functionally illiterate and were unable to read even the word lists they were given. It is quite clear that the majority of our informants have been alienated from the schools and that their values do not coincide with the middle-class values placed on educational achievement. From background information available to us, it appears that many of the informants can be considered integral members of indigenous peer groups, participating fully in the street culture of New York City.

Our contacts with the informants were established through Youth Development, Inc., a club-like organization with recreational facilities such as table billiards, ping pong, and a basketball court open to the public daily. During the summer months, the organization has established camp facilities at Lake Champion, New York, where the same general activities available in the city are offered on an extended level. The fieldwork which serves as a basis for this analysis was conducted at the camp site. Follow-up interviews were also conducted with some of the informants in East Harlem.

The informants were not chosen randomly. Rather, a decision was made to start interviewing several informants who had considerable status among their peers. This decision was calculated in order to facilitate other interviews and to give us some sample of peer groups. It was anticipated that other individuals would recognize that the leaders had been chosen initially, and that to be asked for an interview would then be associated with status. It was further reasoned that positive reports from informants initially would enhance our chances of obtaining interviews with other informants.

Although somewhat of a risk (since negative reports by leaders would seriously hinder further interviewing), the procedure proved to be generally quite successful in obtaining informants. The association of the interviews with peer status apparently was understood by other members. In fact, several peer associates of our original contacts asked to talk to us before we had an opportunity to request an interview.

After establishing contacts with several of the peer leaders, we selected informants either on the basis of our acquaintance with them through informal contact, reference to other individuals from our initial interviews, recommendation from workers who knew the informants through more extensive interaction on a day to day basis, or a combination of these.

As a first step in looking at the linguistic assimilation of Black English among second-generation Puerto Rican teenagers in Harlem, it is necessary to separate Puerto Rican informants on the basis of their social interactions with blacks. There are a number of criteria which we might use for classifying Puerto Ricans into various groups with respect to their contacts with blacks, and in our more detailed study (Wolfram et al. 1971) we have examined several of them. It is clear that the most crucial of these is peer contacts. Who do they associate with in their friendship groups in the neighborhood? In order to elicit this information, each informant was asked to list his main friendship groups and to identify the race of the each individual member of that group. The information elicited by this procedure was compared with observation by staff members who were familiar with the informants over an extended period and our participant observation of social interactions during the fieldwork. Although there is obviously a continuum with respect to the extent of black contacts revealed by our informants, we have chosen to separate informants into two groups on the basis of our sociological information: those with extensive black contacts and those with restricted black contacts. Those with extensive black contacts indicate a mixed or majority of blacks among their peers while those with restricted contacts have few or no blacks in their immediate peer groups. The types of group structures, initiation into peer groups, and the activities of the peer groups all give supportive information for our assessment (cf. Wolfram et al. 1971 for further detail on these assessments).

Parameters of language assimilation. There are a number of different vantage points from which we may view language or dialect assimilation. We may, for example, look at the assimilation of particular linguistic items by the speech communities in contact. This is the traditional way in which linguists have looked at the effects of linguistic systems in contact. We may also, however, look at communicative acts rather than linguistic items per se. On this level, verbal events such as narrative and conversational types are examined as communities with different verbal 'styles' come into contact. This type of assimilation usually is more apt to be examined by the ethnographer than the linguist, since it deals with the broader communicative functions of language.

Both of the above aspects of languages in contact can be dealt with from a fairly objective point of view. But languages, or dialects, do not come into contact under neutral emotional conditions. There are always concomitant attitudinal reactions on the part of the groups in contact. This, of course, is a quite different vantage point from that taken by the traditional linguist. Yet, it is an essential correlate of objective language data which must be considered when viewing language assimilation in the broader perspective of language and society.

In the illustrative account that follows, we shall examine the assimilation of black speech by Puerto Ricans in terms of the several different sociolinguistic levels cited above. First, we shall look at the assimilation of particular linguistic features of Black English by Puerto Ricans in New York City. This aspect of the description is based solely on objective data. In this section, the concept of the 'linguistic variable', as used in studies such as Labov's (1966, 1968) Shuy, Wolfram, and Riley (1967), and Wolfram (1969) serves as our general model for description. Frequency tabulation of the variants of a variable are presented as quantitative evidence for assimilation. In the second illustrative description, we shall examine the relative assimilation of certain black verbal activities. In this section, it is the cultural interpretation of verbal activity rather than specific linguistic items which is in focus. The cultural understanding of the form and function of such activities is our concern in this section. This account would probably be considered part of an ethnography of communication, since it deals with the function of communication. In the final section, we shall look at the perception of speech differences on the part of the different Puerto Rican groups. Our description in that section will be based primarily on indirect and open-ended comments by informants rather than on psychometrics. In part, this is due to the fact that the original interviews were not specifically focused on language attitudes. But it also appears that authentic subjective reactions to speech may be more likely when they appear as indirect and open-ended comments rather than forced choices with respect to predetermined categories of reaction.

The assimilation of linguistic items. In order for us to attribute particular linguistic features used by Puerto Ricans in East Harlem to the influence of Black English, it is necessary for us to limit our examination to those items which are unique to Black English among the various dialects used in New York City. Specifically, this means that a number of the items generally described as an integral part of Black English must be eliminated from our consideration. As studies of Black English illustrate, many of the features characteristic of Black English also typify other nonstandard varieties of English. For example, the realization of morpheme-initial đ as d in items like the, they, and that or the frequent absence of post-vocalic r in items like four, sister, and board are phenomena widespread among the various white and black nonstandard varieties of English. To discover its widespread usage among Puerto Ricans does not necessarily indicate that its usage is acquired from blacks. We may interject here that it is not necessary that the features we choose be unique to Black

English when compared with various dialects outside of New York City (e. g. Southern white speech), but only that they be unique among the various dialect options available in the local context.

In addition to our elimination of Black English features shared by other varieties of English spoken in New York City, it is also necessary to eliminate from consideration those features which might occur in Puerto Rican English due to interference from Spanish. We must be careful not to confuse interference and assimilation phenomena. For example, the reduction of certain word-final consonant clusters (e. g. [wes] 'west' [mɛs] 'messed') has sometimes been cited as one of the aspects characteristic of Black English phonology. But consonant cluster reduction of this type may also be a phenomena which is quite predictable on the basis of interference from Puerto Rican Spanish because of the morpheme structure rules of Spanish (Spanish morpheme structure rules do not allow word-final st, nd, kt, etc.). Consonant cluster reduction is a well-known characteristic of Spanish interference, and may be found independent of any of the English dialects with which Puerto Ricans come into contact. The similarity in the realizations from these two sources, referred to elsewhere as 'convergent processes', must be eliminated as primary indicators of assimilation phenomena. [1]

One of the widespread features of Black English which qualifies in terms of the conditions stated above is morpheme-final //θ//. [2] Quite typically, items like tooth, mouth, and Ruth are realized as [tUf], [maUf], and [rUf] respectively. We can look at the distribution of the f variant among the black informants used as a control group and the two groups of Puerto Ricans distinguished previously in Table 1. The tabulation is based on the extraction of variables from the spontaneous conversation of these informants during their initial tape-recorded interview.

TABLE 1. Comparison of f realization in morpheme-final position for Blacks, Puerto Ricans with extensive Black contacts, and Puerto Ricans with limited Black contacts.

	Occ. f	Occ. θ	% f
Black	36	8	81. 8
PR with extensive Black contacts	20	3	87. 0
PR with limited Black contacts	53	44	54. 6

The distribution of $\underline{f}$ realization in the preceding table is quite straightforward. The Puerto Ricans with extensive black contacts match (in fact, they exceed, but not to any significant degree) the extent of $\underline{f}$ realization found among the black informants, while the Puerto Ricans with limited black contacts reveal significantly less $\underline{f}$ realization than both groups. ($X^2 = 7.93$, $p < .01$ when the Puerto Ricans with restricted black contact are compared with the Puerto Ricans with extensive black contacts.)

The same pattern of distribution can be demonstrated by looking at another phonological variable, this time related to the vowel system of Black English. In Black English, there are a number of environments where the upgliding offset of diphthongs can be reduced or deleted, so that we have a centralized glide or a monophthong. Words like time, try, and ride may be realized as [ta⁽ᵊ⁾m], [tra⁽ᵊ⁾], or [ra⁽ᵊ⁾d]. Although this realization is quite common in some southern varieties of white English, it is not typically used in white dialects spoken in northern contexts such as New York City. The distribution of two main variants (i.e. the presence or absence of the upglide) is indicated in Table 2. Although there are a number of linguistic environments where this realization may occur, the table only indicates the incidence of the variants for word-final position. It is in this environment that the $\underline{a}$ variant is most likely to occur for all the groups.[3] Tabulation was made on the basis of the spontaneous conversation of the informants.

TABLE 2. Comparison of $\underline{a}$ realization in word-final position for Blacks, Puerto Ricans with extensive Black contacts, and Puerto Ricans with limited Black contacts.[4]

	Occ. a	Occ. ay	% a
Black	190	57	76.9
PR with extensive Black contacts	104	44	70.3
PR with limited Black contacts	261	396	39.7

The same pattern observed in Table 1 is repeated in Table 2. There is no significant difference between the Black and Puerto Ricans with extensive black contacts with respect to this feature. The Puerto Ricans with restricted black contacts and those with extensive black contacts differ quite significantly (X^2 = 45.47, p < .001).

Although we have clearly demonstrated that there is a significant difference between the two groups of Puerto Ricans with respect to these phonological variables, it is essential to note that the differences are quantitative. That is, we observe a certain amount of black influence on both groups, but the one group simply shows a higher frequency of the assimilated variants. The black influence on both groups of Puerto Rican teenagers may be due to the fact that it is virtually impossible for a Puerto Rican teenager in Harlem to avoid some contact with blacks, despite the fact that he may not include them in his peer group. It may be that this restricted contact is sufficient for the assimilation of Black English features to a limited extent. But even if Puerto Ricans with restricted black contacts do not assimilate phonological features from the sporadic contact that they have with blacks, it is quite reasonable to suggest that some assimilation may be acquired indirectly. That is, Puerto Rican adolescents with restricted black contacts may be assimilating phonological features of black English from Puerto Ricans with more extensive black contacts rather than the blacks themselves.

In the above discussion, we have made no mention of grammatical variables. In order to see if grammatical variables reveal the same type of distribution as the phonological ones we may look at a grammatical feature unique to Black English in New York City.

One of the grammatical features which is considered unique to Black English in New York City is the use of 'distributive be'. This particular grammatical feature has been described by a number of linguists who vary slightly in their analysis, but who generally agree that it refers to a repeated occurrence of some type (cf. Fasold 1969: 746). The distributive function of be is illustrated in sentences such as:

(1) He don't usually be home.
(2) Sometimes he be at home; I know he do.

This particular function of be as a finite form should be distinguished from two other uses which are derived from underlying will be or would be by phonological processes. A sentence like (3) is derived from underlying will be since the negative form of this sentence is (4).

(3) He be here in a few minutes.
(4) He won't be here in a few minutes.

Similarly, sentence (5) is derived from <u>would be</u> since the negative counterpart to (5) requires the modal <u>would</u> in Black English (6).

(5) He be happy if he could come home.
(6) He wouldn't be happy if he could come home.

The occurrences of distributive <u>be</u> as well as <u>be</u> derived from <u>will</u> <u>be</u> or <u>would be</u> are tabulated in Table 3 for representatives from the three groups.[5] In addition, however, another category includes the cases which are ambiguous. Despite considerable contextual clues which often clarify the derivation of <u>be</u>, there still remain some cases where it is impossible to determine the underlying source of <u>be</u>. This is due mainly to the fact that <u>will be</u> can often be used to refer to habitual activity of some type, a meaning which is quite close to the use of distributive <u>be</u> (e.g. <u>Whenever he's around his friends he'll be good</u>).

TABLE 3.   Occurrences of invariant <u>be</u> for blacks, Puerto Ricans with extensive black contacts, and Puerto Ricans with limited black contacts.

	Dist. be/Pot.	% be	Ambiguous	will or would/Pot.
Black	20/53	37.7	6	2/4
PR with extensive Black contacts	7/46	15.2	2	2/9
PR with limited Black contacts	0/33	0.0	1	2/5

The figures in Table 3 clearly indicate the contrast between the groups. Although all three groups indicate several examples of <u>be</u> derived from underlying <u>will be</u> or <u>would be</u>, (the forms derived through phonological processes) only the blacks and Puerto Ricans with extensive black contacts reveal distributive <u>be</u>. The categorical absence of distributive <u>be</u> for the three Puerto Rican informants with restricted black contacts indicates that it is a feature which may not be expected to be assimilated by Puerto Ricans unless they have extensive contacts with blacks.

Although we have only cited an illustrative example here, similar results have been obtained for a number of grammatical features unique to Black English among the nonstandard varieties of New York City (cf. Wolfram et al. 1971, particularly Chapter 4). This observation points to a basic difference in the assimilation of features when they are separated on the basis of phonology and grammar. To some extent, the influence of Black English phonological features is common to both groups of Puerto Ricans, the differences between the groups being quantitative. Grammatical features, however, tend to reveal more qualitative differences between the groups. Whereas phonological features may be assimilated through indirect means or through limited contact with blacks, it is apparent that grammatical features unique to Black English are assimilated only through extensive peer contacts.

At this point, we can only hypothesize as to why phonological features are more subject to widespread assimilation by Puerto Ricans than grammatical ones. One possible reason may relate to the nature of the linguistic levels involved. For one, the units of phonology (i.e. systematic phonemes) are a relatively small, closed set of items which occur, for the most part, with quite high frequency. The restrictions of the inventory and the relatively high frequency with which the unit occurs may make phonological items more susceptible to assimilation through indirect means or restricted contact. Or, we may suggest that the more superficial the level of language involved, the more susceptible it is to borrowing. Since phonological rules operate on a much more superficial level of language than grammatical rules, they are the rules more susceptible to borrowing.

One might also hypothesize that the reason there is a difference in the assimilation of phonological and grammatical phenomena is due to sociocultural reasons. Previous studies of socially diagnostic linguistic variables (cf. Wolfram 1969) indicate that grammatical variables more sharply differentiate social groups than do phonological ones. That is, various social groups are more definitely marked on the basis of grammatical features. Given the fact that Puerto Ricans with restricted black contacts often view linguistic assimilation from blacks negatively (a matter which we shall discuss in more detail later), it may be suggested that the relative obtrusiveness of grammatical features makes them less susceptible to borrowing than less obtrusive phonological ones. [7] Linguistic and sociocultural explanations for the difference in assimilation phenomena are, of course, not mutually exclusive. It is quite possible that they reinforce each other.

The assimilation of verbal activities. In the previous section, we have only dealt with those aspects of assimilation which are accounted for in a 'conventional' linguistic description. That is, they are derived through the application of phonological and grammatical rules. But there is another aspect of language usage not generally accounted for when the description is limited to these types of phenomena; namely, the selection of those items from the speaker's linguistic repertoire which are appropriate for a given social situation. These sorts of phenomena are generally considered to be matters of 'communicative competence' rather than 'linguistic competence' per se. For example, understanding systems of address with respect to the appropriate titles for individuals in a given social relation involves this sort of competence. Competence of this type involves a common knowledge of the function or purpose of the linguistic message on the part of both speaker and hearer.

If the premises of the speaker and hearer are not the same, it is quite possible to misunderstand the function of a message despite the fact that all the phonological and grammatical structures are understood completely. Suppose, for example, a child, in one context, learned that adults with whom he was friendly could be addressed on a first name basis. An adult, in another context, associates children's use of first names for adults as disrespective of adult roles and considers it appropriate for children to address adults only by their last name. If the child assumes that he is indicating his friendship to the adult by addressing him on a first name basis while the adult considers this an insult, we have an obvious gap in communicative content. This breakdown may occur despite the fact that both the addresser and addressee share a common competence in syntactic and phonological content. In some respects, variations in communicative competence across subcultures may lead to more serious communication breakdowns than variations in the linguistic items per se. In this section we shall look at one aspect of communicative competence as a potential indicator of assimilation among the Puerto Rican groups in East Harlem.

One of the characteristic aspects of lower socioeconomic black adolescent vernacular culture is the use of language in a prescribed and ceremonial fashion; that is, there are ritualistic patterns for certain types of verbal interactions. The ritualistic use of language has been described for black adolescent males in Harlem in detail by Labov et al. (1968, Vol. II); it has also been described in other urban contexts by Abrahams (1963), Kochman (1968), and Kerman (1969). Probably the most well known of these rituals is what is commonly called by our black informants, sounding (sometimes, it is also referred to as 'the dozens', but the use of this term is apparently decreasing). Other terms are also in use in other urban settings. To describe it briefly (for more detail see Labov et al. 1968:2.76-129), the activity is generally thought of in terms of insulting someone's mother, although other relatives might also be mentioned (e. g. grandmother, father, uncle). The presuppositions under which the activity is conducted are shared by the participants; namely, that the

insult is not literally true. The proper cultural response to a ritualistic insult is another ritualistic insult. Typically, sounding takes
place between two participants; but others are spectators and become
judges of the quality of a sound (by laughter, jeering, or comments).
The informal judging of such events should not be underestimated; it
becomes clear who has the upper hand. The first participant initially
insults someone's mother, and the respondent attempts to 'outdo' him
by responding with an insult that evokes a more effective response with
the audience. Trading insults may stop at any stage, but effective
sounders can trade verbal quips at some length. This verbal ritual
may involve a number of topics, but probably the most prominent ones
deal with the mother's sexual activity. Other topics include poverty,
age, and physical attributes (skin color, weight, age, etc.).

During the course of our fieldwork, we had considerable opportunity to observe interactions involving ritualistic language usage and
each informant was interviewed about this topic. On the basis of this
information we can discuss the verbal activity of sounding as it is an
indicator of linguistic-cultural assimilation of black culture by Puerto
Ricans. For the indigenous member of black culture, reference to
this activity involves (1) an understanding of the procedural guidelines
(i.e. the structure of the conversation exchange between interlocutors),
(2) the function of the activity (i.e. its ritualistic rather than literal
intention), (3) and the informal rules governing the content (i.e.
topics and persons who can be the object of sounding). Obviously,
there is a wide range of skill represented by various members of the
community. This is to be expected. For our purposes, we are more
concerned with informants' cultural understanding of the activity than
their actual verbal skill.

While sounding is widespread and a highly developed ritual among
many indigenous black groups of adolescent males, there is no cultural analogue for this activity in traditional Puerto Rican culture.
This, of course, is not to say that there is no type of joking behavior
or that ritualistic insults cannot occur. It is simply to say that the
verbal activity that we described above does not have a specific
analogue in traditional Puerto Rican culture. In fact, ritualistic insults of mothers and relatives as it occurs in sounding are generally
considered taboo behavior. Mothers are not candidates for insults
either ritualistically or literally. To insult a mother is to 'curse'
her, and this type of activity may readily lead to hostility between
the insulter and the mother's son.

Because there is considerable cultural difference in how this
activity may be interpreted by blacks and Puerto Ricans from traditional Puerto Rican culture, the observation of informants' reactions to this activity may be an important marker of Puerto Rican
assimilation of black verbal styles. We may hypothesize that the

Puerto Rican informants with many black peers will characteristically understand more of the rules for this activity and its cultural function as a ritualistic activity. First, of course, we expect that they should be familiar with how the activity proceeds. Our Puerto Rican informants with extensive black contacts quite typically indicate this knowledge. Consider, for example, the following exchange with one of these informants. The following excerpt should be prefaced by noting that the informant had previously been observed in extensive sounding sessions and had been reputed to have considerable verbal skill in the activity. (The fieldworker had also established quite good rapport with the informant through participation in a number of activities with him before the interview.)

FW: You're a pretty good sounder I hear. What if somebody said to you, 'your mother drink pee'.

Inf: Your mother's a wino, tell you like that.

FW: Your mother's name Annie Oakley.

Inf: Your mother steal life preservers from Eastern Airlines.

FW: Your mother so old she fart dust.

Inf: Say your mother so old everytime she snap her fingers she crack her knuckles.

FW: What if I said your mother's like a railroad track, she been laid all over the country?

Inf: Say your mother got more tracks than canal 47.

FW: What if I said your mother got legs coming out her nose?

Inf: Your mother got laid so many time she look like hopeless hoe (5:8-9). [8]

In the above passage, the informant obviously demonstrates that he understands how the exchange of the discourse is structured. He further indicates that he is familiar with the topics which are suitable for ritualistic insult and the type of response which can 'score' (i. e. bring about a positive effect as indicated by the evaluation of the peer participants). That is, he keeps the topic constant (i.e. if the participant insults his mother, his response is in terms of his mother) while elaborating on the theme of the comment (e.g. the insult 'Your mother so old she fart dust' is responded to by the comment 'your mother so old every time she snap her fingers she crack her knuckles'). Although some of the other Puerto Rican informants with extensive black contact do not show the same degree of verbal skill in this activity, it is still quite obvious from their comments that they are quite familiar with how the activity proceeds. Consider, for example, the following excerpts.

Inf: Yeah, like yesterday we went over there and this guy name Rollie, me and him was sounding about mothers, you know, say 'Hey man, your mother's a cab driver, no your mother this and that' . . . We joke with him like that and he came back with it, ah man, 'Your mother this and how's your mother', and I say, 'Oh yeah, your father too', we just keep it up, and then we stop and we shake hands, see that's the way I like people, don't take things serious.

FW: What would you say if Rollie said, 'Your mother's a cab driver'?

Inf: I'll say your mother's a bus driver.

FW: What if he says your mother stink?

Inf: And your mother's a box, we gotta lot of ways to it.

FW: Your mother drink pee.

Inf: . . . I said that I got to your mother and then he say, 'Your mother's a hole', and I tell him, 'Your father's a faggot' and we kept on, but we never took it serious (18: 6-7).

Again there is obvious familiarity with the activity on the part of the informant. The procedure of the verbal exchange and the informal rules governing topics and comments is again illustrated, although this informant does not have the reputation for his skill that we indicated for the previously cited informant. Also indicated in the above passage, is a cultural understanding of its ritualistic rather than its literal intent. Comments like 'we never took it serious' and 'that's the way I like people, don't take it so serious' in the above passage are references to this cultural understanding. It is quite plain, then, that the informal rules and cultural function of this verbal activity have been assimilated by Puerto Rican adolescent males with extensive black contacts.

Now let us turn to the Puerto Rican group with restricted black contacts. With respect to the type of discourse involved in sounding, a majority of our informants indicated that they were quite familiar with the activity, although, in some cases, the term was not immediately related to the activity by the informants.

FW: What about sounding?

Inf: . . . Oh yeah, sounding, you mean like, you know, your mother eats . . .

FW: What did you think I meant?

Inf: I thought you meant cursing.

FW: What if I said your mother smelled like twenty pounds of yesterday?

Inf: Your father.

FW: What would be an example of one with a curse in it?

Inf: Well, your mother has hair on her chest, your father has a pussy, and, you know, all that silly stuff (7:1).

Typically, informants are familiar with the procedural guide lines which govern this activity, but they do not spend nearly as much time engaged in the verbal activity as blacks or Puerto Rican informants with extensive black contacts. There are, however, several of the informants who indicate practically no familiarity with it, as illustrated by the following exchange with one informant.

FW: I hear a lot of sounding. Is sounding . . . ?

Inf: Like the way you talk?

FW: No, you know, sounding on each other.

Inf: Or like we're cursing at each other or something?

FW: Like if somebody said your mother has BO or something like that.

Inf: Oh yeah, body odor.

FW: What if they said your mother wears combat boots or your mother drinks pee?

Inf: No, that don't have nothing to do with it.

FW: Do you ever do any of it? Like, I hear a lot of it around here.

Inf: Like we do it, but they don't do it, you know . . . Like if you want to crack a little bit of jokes, you know, if you want to laugh, you know, my friend Izzie comes out with some good jokes (34:11).

This type of response is more typical of Puerto Rican informants who are somewhat oriented toward the values of mainstream culture (as indicated by educational achievement, aspiration, peer group activities, etc.) vis-a-vis the indigenous street culture. That is, they are cultural 'lames'. This term, obviously borrowed from the contiguous black community, is used by informants themselves to describe either a social isolate who does not have extensive peer contacts or an individual who has peer contacts with a group that maintains values which conflict with the values of the indigenous culture. Although, as a part of this study, we interviewed several black informants who might qualify as lames, we may note that there was considerably more familiarity indicated by these informants than the Puerto Rican lames. The degree of unfamiliarity indicated above is not typical of the responses of the group as a whole. (Only three other informants in this group indicated this extent of unfamiliarity.) Generally speaking, we may conclude that Puerto Ricans with restricted black contacts are familiar with the form of the verbal exchange.

For the most part, the content is also familiar to the majority of Puerto Rican informants with restricted black contacts. That is, the topics we described previously as usually represented in sounding are verified by the informants. There is, however, one interesting restriction on the content indicated by several of the informants. These informants limit or redefine sounding so that mothers may be eliminated as topics for insult. This sort of restriction is indicated in the comments that follow.

Inf: Everybody sounds sometime. Like if somebody has a pair
of funny sneakers or something, then you, like start making
jokes at it or like if once you were playing a game and you
fell or something, they start, they bring it up and start
laughing at it then everybody keeps on making more things.

FW: Do they sound on mothers?

Inf: No, 'cause some people's mothers are dead and like once
this guy sound at his mother and the guy started crying and
got mad and he was going to hit him with a bottle 'cause they
don't like nobody cursing at they mothers (33:7).

FW: Do they sound on someone's mother?

Inf: No, very seldom, no only on ourself. We don't talk about
people's mothers . . . 'cause if somebody starts cussing on
people's mother, you know, if they want to have a fight I
got a pair boxing gloves (43:8).

It may be hypothesized that mothers are eliminated from the ritualistic insults because of the influence of the traditional Puerto Rican
taboo on such insults. The general activity may be adopted, but it
is modified in such a way as to make it more compatible with traditional Puerto Rican culture. Rather than take the risk of having the
ritualistic insult misinterpreted with respect to traditional Puerto
Rican culture, the topic of mothers simply may be eliminated.
Where there is not adaptation of the type mentioned above, we have
a situation which may be subject to cross-cultural misunderstanding.
The hostility that can be aroused if the functional intent is not precisely understood is a recurrent theme in the comments of the majority of Puerto Ricans with restricted black contacts. In several
of the quotes mentioned above, sounding is associated with 'cursing
someone's mother', and we have already stressed the seriousness of
this offense. We have many references to fights which have occurred
as a result of the apparent misunderstanding of the function of sounding. Comments like the following are recurrent throughout our interviews with informants in this category.

FW: Do the guys sound on one another?

Inf: They usually do, man, ah like they be sounding on they
mothers like that all they could think of mothers and your
mother is this and that and that could really get a guy angry,
you don't have no right of sounding on mines . . .

FW: What if somebody said your mother drinks pee?

Inf: I would punch them in the mouth for that or otherwise I
would tell them to keep his cool (11:7-8).

Our references to hostile activity resulting from sounding among
some of the Puerto Ricans with restricted black contacts should not,
of course, be taken to mean that hostilities never arise among blacks
or Puerto Ricans with extensive black contacts. Hostilities can
arise for a number of reasons (e.g. a sound is not sufficiently so
that it can allow a literal rather than ritualistic interpretation or an
opponent is sufficiently outdone so as to react hostilely out of em-
barrassment or frustration) among the other groups. But we are im-
pressed by the recurrency of this theme in the comments of the Puerto
Ricans with restricted black contacts as compared with the occasional,
and usually, tangential, mention of tensions surrounding the activity by
the other groups. We may hypothesize that the obsession with the
hostilities surrounding this activity are related to the potential for
cross-cultural misinterpretation. Familiarity with the procedural
guidelines of the verbal activity obviously does not necessarily insure
understanding of its cultural function.

The preceding illustrative description demonstrates that a thorough
account of language assimilation must consider communicative as well
as linguistic competence. These types of verbal activity may be
diagnostic of assimilation in a manner which parallels the more traditional examination of linguistic variables. And, as we have stated
earlier, the examination of verbal activities may be just as important,
if not more so, than the examination of linguistic items in our description of language or dialects in contact.

The subjective level of language assimilation. In the previous
descriptions of linguistic assimilation, we have focused primarily on
objective aspects of language (although, of course, some of our
description of language repertoire in the previous section was based
on informants' perceptions of specific verbal activities). In this
section we shall look at some aspects of the more general perception
of the language situation on the part of the Puerto Rican groups. The
previous descriptive sections have given us an idea of what type of
language assimilation is taking place. Now we want to know how Puerto
Ricans view and react to the linguistic assimilation in a wider cultural framework. As with the other descriptive accounts, we are
dependent on interviews with the informants and observation of
various language contact situations on by the informants.

To begin with, we must observe that there is a tendency for Puerto
Ricans with extensive black contacts to minimize differences that

exist between groups. We may thus get informants in this group who
deny that the way blacks and Puerto Ricans speak English is different.
For some of these informants, there is, of course, a great deal of
objective similarity in the variety of English used by the two groups.
But informants who would still perceptually be identified as being
Puerto Rican may also tend to minimize these differences. The
tendency to minimize speech differences that we observe on the part
of Puerto Ricans is consistent with their perception of the social relations of these groups in a wider context. For example, we have
observed that informants in this category may minimize physical
differences between the groups, as one informant noted:

> It's really hard to tell between a Puerto Rican and a Negro;
> it's really hard, you know (18:second interview).

Similarly, social tensions between the communities may be minimized.

> You know, like before, it was a lot of race problem in East
> Harlem, like the community works together, you know, none
> of this bullshit about now, you black, get away from me,
> you're white, you better go to Hell or something like that.
> Ain't like that no more, you know (5:7).

In reality, of course, there are considerably more differences
than are admitted in the above comment. For example, a member of
the Puerto Rican community generally would have little difficulty in
distinguishing the blacks from the Puerto Ricans. And we know that
there are still many tensions which exist between the black and Puerto
Rican communities. For our purposes here, however, the actual
situation is less important than the perception of social relations by
Puerto Ricans in this category.

An interesting assessment of the unity of blacks and Puerto Ricans
by the members of this group has been observed in relation to the use
of Spanish in peer group situations. In questioning about the use of
Spanish with friends, several informants cited the fact that blacks
learn to speak Spanish. One informant made the following observation
when he was asked if any of the members of his peer spoke Spanish.

> Inf: Yeah, mostly the colored guys.

> FW: The colored guys speak Spanish? Do you speak Spanish with
> one another?

> Inf: You know, like sometime I say, 'tu madre es puta', that
> means your mother's a whore, and the guy says, 'tu abuela'

you know, 'your grandmother' and jive, and they say, 'Vamos a comer', let's go eat', stuff like that, yeah, and they know how to say like, somebody be talking, like two parents be talking, they say, 'Estos ninos son tecatos', you know, like these kids are junkies, and they go around and they say, Hey man, your mother's over there saying we're junkies, I heard her, something like that (5:11).

Another informant in this category confirms this impression when he says, 'Colored dudes, you know, they know Spanish too' (18:second interview). In reality, we find that the extent of Spanish usage found among blacks in these peer groups is generally restricted to a few phrases or lexical items. One of the black informants in our corpus gives an illustration of this phenomenon when he is talking about a Puerto Rican who is a member of a predominantly black peer group.

We say like, 'Eh mira', you know, we talk in Spanish and ask him for a cigarette, 'Dame cigarillo' and he say I don't have none and he say, 'look here', man, he make his speech, like if we have a party or something and that guy say, 'Look at that Spanish guy over there' he walk over to him, he say, he make his little speech, he say, 'Listen now, listen to me real good, I may be Spanyola on the outside, but inside I have a Negro heart, you know'. Everybody look at him and say, you know, they start clapping, they say, 'Reuben, say some more', and he be telling all that and then you know, most the time they say, 'what's happening', you know, he consider hisself a Nigger, I wouldn't blame him (1:17).

It is obvious from other comments by Puerto Ricans and our observation of social interactions that the claim concerning the acquisition of Spanish by blacks is quite exaggerated. The learning of a few fixed phrases is quite different from acquiring language competence in Puerto Rican Spanish. Statements by Puerto Rican informants also tend to contradict their observation that blacks speak Spanish. In other contexts, Puerto Ricans mention that Spanish is generally avoided around black peers. The reasons for this avoidance are stated succinctly by one Puerto Rican with extensive black peers who observes that the reason he does not use Spanish with his peers is 'So the guy could know that I'm boss, I don't want to hide nothing'. For Puerto Ricans to use Spanish with black peers is socially inappropriate since it may be associated with ineptness in cultural adaptation. As illustrated in the previously cited quote, Puerto Ricans with predominantly black peers have to prove that they belong. The use of Spanish with another Puerto Rican in the peer group would thus be counterproductive to this purpose. Furthermore, the use of Spanish may be disruptive to a social group. If a black peer does not understand it, he may view it suspiciously, in which case it could be disruptive to the social group. Informants mentioned that Puerto Ricans who talk Spanish around black peers may be suspected of criticizing or attempting to conceal information from their black peers.

If Spanish is not likely to be used around black peers, we may ask why some of the Puerto Ricans make special mention of the fact that blacks speak Spanish. Part of the reason may be related to the point that was mentioned earlier; that is, the tendency of Puerto Ricans with extensive black contacts to minimize differences that exist between the two groups. But we may also hypothesize that there is a desire on the part of these informants to interpret assimilation as reciprocal. That is, not only are Puerto Ricans assimilating aspects of the surrounding black culture, but blacks are also assimilating aspects of Puerto Rican culture. In reality, assimilation is largely one-way; it is the Puerto Ricans who are copying the blacks. Black teen-agers do not pick up aspects of Puerto Rican English which might identify them as being Puerto Rican, such as occasional syllable-timing, the tendency not to reduce vowels in unstressed syllables, and so forth. Nor do they pick up any real conversational ability in Puerto Rican Spanish. When more integrative aspects of linguistic competence are considered, the few phrases or lexical items learned by some blacks in East Harlem must be considered tokens. These sorts of phrases indicate a relatively superficial level of borrowing. But these small tokens apparently are interpreted quite symbolically by some Puerto Ricans who desire to see the assimilation process working both ways.

Now let us turn to the Puerto Ricans with restricted black contacts. Unlike the Puerto Ricans with extensive black peer group contacts, there is no tendency to minimize the speech differences between the groups. Therefore, we find informants in this category perceiving blacks and Puerto Ricans as talking quite differently. The following types of reactions are quite typical.

FW: Is there a difference between the way Puerto Ricans and blacks talk?
Inf: Say, like a white person, he will say, 'you try to be cool', now a black person will say, 'You all try to be cool'. So there's an accent right there (39:second interview).

FW: Is there any difference between the way Puerto Ricans and blacks talk?

Inf: Yes, there is a big difference . . . Spanish, he'll say slap me five, but the Negro will come up and say, 'Put some skin on my hand', you know, and he'll use 'man' and he'll say, 'Come on, man, let's go and do our little thing'.

FW: Puerto Ricans don't say that, right?

Inf: They say it, but it's different, way different by the way Negroes say it (43:second interview).

FW: Do you think that black and Puerto Ricans sound any different when they talk?

Inf: Yeah, I think the Negro stretches the word.

FW: Give me an example of him stretching the word.

Inf: Like when they say man I would say, 'Hey man, cut it out'. Listening to a Negro, they don't speak like that, they say, 'maaan', and it starts moving you know. They emphasize on the word more (11:second interview).

This perception of speech differences is consistent with the perception of differences between blacks and Puerto Ricans in East Harlem on a broader cultural level. Despite the fact that the social position of Puerto Ricans and blacks is quite similar in the wider context of American society, there is sometimes considerable intergroup tension. This tension tends to highlight the differences between the groups.

You see, we have half a building full of niggers, guys that really look for trouble. They all came down 'round about and a couple of guys from our building and we have room. 8 [sic] per cent of the guys round here are Spanish. They surrounded the niggers on the outside I went straight down and hit a couple of them on the head. Now I was at the bottom and when the Spanish finished with the niggers out there, they came in. They don't fool around with the Spanish cause, what you call it, Spanish take their ass and make it inside out (43:13-14).

These types of tensions are not uncommon, despite superficial statements of solidarity about the relations between the groups.

Like some of these Negro guys, I don't hang around, most of the guys that stick around there, they always, you know, look for trouble (35:9).

In such a context, then, it is quite predictable that differences in speech should be brought out to parallel the perception of other social differences.

At this point, we must remember that Puerto Ricans with restricted black contacts, despite their perception of speech differences, do show some influence in certain aspects of their speech. We have shown that there is some phonological influence regardless of the extent of contact. If we had included vocabulary in our study, we would also have seen that there are a number of indigenous black terms which have been borrowed into the lexicon of both groups of Puerto Ricans. But these similarities are perceived as insignificant when compared with the amount of assimilation revealed by Puerto Ricans with extensive black contacts. In fact, there is evidence, that some Puerto Ricans are not conscious of the extent to which black speech may have influenced their own speech. This was vividly illustrated in one incident that occurred following an interview. The informant, never having heard his voice on a tape recorder, asked to play back part of the interview. After listening to his voice for a minute, he worriedly exclaimed to the interviewer, 'Man, I sound just like a nigger'. The assimilation of Black English may be viewed negatively by Puerto Ricans in this group, despite the fact that they have assimilated aspects of Black English in their own speech. Consider the following comments in this connection.

FW: Do a lotta Spanish kids sound like black kids?
Inf: Sometimes . . .
FW: How about you? Do you think you ever sound like a black when you talk?
Inf: I don't know, do I?
FW: I want your opinion. Do you think you'd like to?
Inf: No.
FW: Why not?
Inf: I want to talk like I always talk. I don't care if I can talk English, at least I can talk.
FW: Do you think that when a Spanish guy talks like a black guy that makes him sound cool?
Inf: Corny.
FW: Does it make him sound tough?
Inf: Not tough but corny.
FW: You know some guys who talk that way?
Inf: Yeah . . . I think they're trying to show off, like, if they got a colored friend, they want to show off in front of him. [9]

The extensive adoption of Black English by Puerto Ricans with extensive black contacts may be viewed as an attempt to be something that a Puerto Rican naturally is not, and therefore be considered pretentious. And even though Puerto Ricans with restricted black contacts may be further removed from traditional Puerto Rican culture than their parents, they may define it as a symbol of the rejection of the Puerto Rican community of which they are still a part.

Any negative reactions toward the assimilation of Black English on the part of the teenagers with restricted black contacts are clearly reinforced in the homes. If parents perceive certain aspects of their children's English to be influenced by black speech, they may react quite negatively. In the first place, many parents speak to their children in Spanish, and may require that the children answer them in Spanish. As it was put by one informant:

> Well, I have to [answer his parents in Spanish]. My father asks
> me a question in Spanish. He won't take it in English. I have
> to answer him in Spanish 'cause he says I'm not an Italian and
> I'm not a Negro, but I'm a Puerto Rican and have to speak to
> me in my language . . . [He says] I was born in Puerto Rico
> and . . . I'm gonna raise you like Puerto Ricans. So if we
> speak English, in front of him . . . it's like cursing right in
> front of him (10:9).

In some instances, it is considered inappropriate for children to answer parents in English at all. To speak to parents in a dialect of English that is discernibly influenced by Black English is to elicit an even stronger reaction on the part of parents. One informant explained how a friend who talked like a black was smacked by his father who said 'You can talk English, but normal English'. There is considerable evidence that the parents view the acquisition of Black English features on the part of their children as quite insulting. The adoption of these features may be interpreted symbolically by a parent as a move away from traditional Puerto Rican culture.

The reactions of Puerto Ricans with restricted black contacts may be summarized as being basically ambivalent. On the one hand, they are quite aware of the differences that exist between the two groups in a number of areas of culture and they tend to perceive these differences in speech as in other areas. On the other hand, they are faced with the reality of the social situation in which it is very difficult to avoid some influence from the black community which surrounds them. By perceiving the amount of influence on their own speech as insignificant they do not have to deal with this limited assimilation while reacting negatively toward the amount of assimilation that takes place among the counterparts with extensive black contacts.

NOTES

[1]Although convergent processes cannot be considered primary indicators of linguistic assimilation from Black English, the frequency distribution of these types of phenomena do differ for those Puerto Ricans with extensive black contacts and those with restricted black contacts (cf. Wolfram 1972).

[2]The double slant lines (//) indicate an underlying phonological representation. Although we shall not discuss it here, there is considerable evidence to indicate that $//\theta//$ underlies some surface realization of morpheme-final [f] in Black English (cf. Fasold 1969: 81).

[3]There is a consistent ordering of environments which increase the probability of a for all the groups, but this shall not be considered here (cf. Wolfram et al. 1971:156-64).

[4]Marie Shiels Djouadi is responsible for the extraction and tabulation of this variable.

[5]For this tabulation, only nine informants were used (three black, three Puerto Rican with extensive black contacts, and three Puerto Ricans with limited black contacts).

[6]Further investigation of the relation of grammatical and phonological assimilation reveals that Black English grammatical processes are assimilated as grammatical processes and phonological processes as phonological ones. At first glance, this may seem like a trivial observation, but a closer examination of some of the features which might be interpreted to result from either grammatical or phonological processes indicates that this is a significant observation (cf. Wolfram 1972:37-40).

[7]One of the arguments against this hypothesis comes from our observation of lexical borrowing. It is generally assumed that socially diagnostic lexical items are more obtrusive than both phonological and grammatical ones. Yet there is considerable lexical borrowing by both groups of Puerto Ricans.

[8]The citation refers to the tape number assigned to the informant in our corpus and the page of the typescript on which the quote may be found. In cases where we have not transcribed the section quoted, we simply give the tape number and which interview we are quoting (i.e. our first or second interview with the informant).

[9]This quote is excerpted from a supplemental series of interviews on Puerto Rican English by Paul Anisman. I am grateful to Mr. Anisman for bringing it to my attention.

REFERENCES

Abrahams, Roger D. 1963. Deep down in the jungle. Chicago, Aldine.

Fasold, Ralph W. 1969. Orthography in reading materials for Black English speaking children. In: Teaching black children to read. Ed. by Joan C. Baratz and Roger W. Shuy. Washington, D. C., Center for Applied Linguistics.

_____. 1969. Tense and the form be in Black English. Language. 45.763-77.

_____. 1971. Minding your Z's and D's: distinguishing syntactic and phonological variable rules. Papers from Seventh Regional Meeting of the Chicago Linguistic Society.

Kochman, Thomas. 1969. Rapping in the black ghetto. Trans-Action.

Labov, William. 1966. The social stratification of English in New York City. Washington, D. C., Center for Applied Linguistics.

_____, Paul Cohen, Clarence Robins, and John Lewis. 1968. A study of the non-standard English of Negro and Puerto Rican speakers in New York City. Final Report, Cooperative Research Project No. 3288, Office of Education.

Mills, C. Wright, Clarence Senior, and Rose Kahn Golsen. 1950. The Puerto Rican journey. New York, Russell and Russell.

Mitchell-Kernan, Claudia. 1969. Language behavior in black urban community. Unpublished Ph. D. dissertation, University of California, Berkeley.

Rand, Christopher. 1958. The Puerto Ricans. New York, Oxford University Press.

Shuy, Roger W., Walter A. Wolfram, and William K. Riley. 1967. Linguistic correlates of social stratification in Detroit speech. Final Report, Cooperative Research Project No. 6-1347, United States Office of Education.

Wolfram, Walt. 1969. A sociolinguistic description of Detroit Negro speech. Washington, D. C., Center for Applied Linguistics.

_____, in collaboration with Marie Shiels and Ralph Fasold. 1971. Overlapping influences in the English of second-generation Puerto Rican teenagers in Harlem. Final Report, Office of Education, Grant No. 3-70-003(508).

_____. 1972. Overlapping influence and linguistic assimilation in second-generation Puerto Rican English. In: Sociolinguistics in cross-cultural analysis. Ed. by David M. Smith and Roger W. Shuy. Washington, D. C., Georgetown University Press.

TEACHERS' ATTITUDES TOWARD BLACK AND
NONSTANDARD ENGLISH AS MEASURED BY THE
LANGUAGE ATTITUDE SCALE[1]

ORLANDO L. TAYLOR

Federal City College and Center for Applied Linguistics

Introduction. Teachers' handling of classroom language problems,
especially those occurring in classrooms with large numbers of 'nonstandard' speakers, is probably influenced greatly by their attitudes
toward a number of topics, including language and cultural differences. Because of this, the claim could be made that language interaction between teachers and students in schools with substantial black
and other minority group children would be better understood by comparing teachers' actions with their professed attitudes toward nonstandard language generally, and Black English in particular. Despite admitted problems in obtaining the 'true' feelings of people on
any subject, it is possible that language attitude data can assist in
determining some of the underlying bases of classroom language
problems related to language differences.

One approach used by the author to assess teachers' attitudes on
language differences has involved the development and administration
of a Language Attitude Scale (LAS). The scale was designed to
solicit data on what teachers think about nonstandard and Black English, and how (or if) this dialect should be used in the classroom.

Description of LAS. LAS is a Lickert-type scaling instrument.
As such, it involves self-evaluation of opinions, in five gradations,
on a set of language statements.[2]

There are two forms of LAS. Each form contains twenty-five items distributed as follows across four content categories:

	# Pro Black English items	# Con Black English items
(1) The structure and inherent usefulness of nonstandard and Black English dialects	4	4
(2) Consequences of using and accepting nonstandard and Black English in the educational setting	4	4
(3) Philosophies concerning the use and acceptance of nonstandard and Black English dialects	4	4
(4) Cognitive and intellectual abilities of speakers or speakers of nonstandard and Black English	—	1
Total	12	13

The items on each of the forms were selected from an initial pool of 117 items as a function of their ability to discriminate teachers with positive Black English attitudes from those with negative Black English attitudes. Judgments of item sensitivity were made following administration of the 117 items to a group of 186 teachers from throughout the United States on the basis of response patterns on each item of the most Pro Black English teachers (top 25%) versus those of the most Con Black English teachers (bottom 25%). Score differences between these two extreme groups were analyzed by means of the t-test. All of the items selected for the two forms of LAS elicited statistically significant response differences at or beyond the .05 confidence level and, indeed, were among those items which elicited the highest t-scores for all of the items within a given content and Pro Black English/Con Black English category. Also, t-values for items were closely matched across forms of LAS. The twenty-five items selected for each form of LAS, together with their t-values, are presented as a function of the four content categories in Tables 1 and 2.[3]

For statistical purposes, an arbitrary scoring system was adopted for coding subjects' responses to LAS items. The system assigned numerical values to responses as follows:

(a) 1 point for strong disagreement with a positive statement;
(b) 2 points for mild disagreement with a positive statement;
(c) 5 points for strong agreement with a positive statement;
(d) 4 points for mild agreement with a positive statement;
(e) 1 point for strong agreement with a negative statement;
(f) 2 points for mild agreement with a negative statement;
(g) 5 points for strong disagreement with a negative statement;
(h) 4 points for mild disagreement with a negative statement; and
(i) 3 points for any no opinion response.

Administration of LAS to a nationwide group of teachers. Numerous assertions have been made about teachers' attitudes toward language behavior and variety, especially as related to Black English. To date, no controlled study has been reported which discusses, in-depth, teachers' attitudes on the various questions which might be related to the topic of nonstandard and Black English. Further, teachers' attitudes on these subjects have not been presented as a function of such variables as race, sex, age, geography, teaching experience, grade taught, etc. LAS was administered to a large cross section of teachers to obtain data of these types.

Methodology

Subjects. A total of 422 teachers were selected for the survey in the following manner. First, one rural and one large urban school system were randomly picked from each of nine Federal Census districts--New England, Middle Atlantic, South Atlantic, East North Central, East South Central, West North Central, West South Central, Mountain, and Pacific.[4] Second, at least twenty teachers (ten males and ten females) were selected in each of the settings in such a way that the racial and cultural compositions of the communities were reflected.

Materials. Form 1 of the Language Attitude Scale was administered to all teachers in the presentation order indicated in Table 3.

Scoring. Ss' responses to each LAS item were scored as described above.

TABLE 1. Items for Form 1 of LAS and their t-values as a function of content and Pro/Con Black English categories.

Content and Pro/Con Black English categories	t-values	Statements
1+	11.4320	Black English sounds as good as Standard English
	7.6299	Black English is cool.
1-	10.8797	Black English is an inferior language system.
	8.1893	Black English is too imprecise to be an effective means of communication.
2+	10.7057	The encouragement of Black English would be beneficial to our national interests.
	10.8535	Societal acceptance of Black English is important for development of self-esteem among black people.
	12.1888	When teachers reject the native language of a student, they do him great harm.
	13.3329	If use of Black English were encouraged, speakers of Black English would be more motivated to achieve academically.
2-	9.4058	It would be detrimental to our country's social welfare if use of Black English became socially acceptable.
	9.2400	The continued use of a nonstandard dialect of English accomplishes nothing worthwhile for an individual.
	10.0289	Allowing and accepting the use of nonstandard English in the classroom will retard the academic progress of of the class.
	8.6754	A decline in the use of nonstandard English dialects would have a positive influence on social unity.

TABLE 1. Continued.

Content and Pro/Con Black English categories	t-values	Statements
3+	10.7609	There is much danger involved in accepting Black English.
	13.3749	Widespread acceptance of Black English is imperative.
	10.0014	A child should not be corrected by teachers for speaking his native non-standard dialect.
	9.4497	We should encourage the continued use of nonstandard English dialects.
3-	10.5426	It is ridiculous to encourage children to speak Black English.
	11.3447	One of the goals of the American school system should be the standardization of the English language.
	9.7386	Teachers have a duty to insure that students do not speak nonstandard dialects of English in the classroom.
	14.6180	Black English should be discouraged.
4-	7.9709	A black child's use of Black English thwarts his ability to learn.

TABLE 2. Items for Form 2 of LAS and their t-values as a
function of content and Pro/Con Black English
categories.

Content and Pro/Con Black English categories	t-values	Statements
+	9.8320	Black English is a clear, thoughtful, and expressive language.
	8.8513	Nonstandard English is as effective for communication as is Standard English.
-	10.3585	Black English is a poorly structured system of language.
	8.5710	Complex concepts cannot be expressed easily through nonstandard dialects like Black English.
2+	10.7042	Black English should be encouraged because it is an important part of black cultural identity.
	11.1051	Acceptance of Black English by teachers is vitally necessary for the welfare of the country.
	12.0885	To reject Black English is to reject an important aspect of the self-identity of black people.
	13.0718	Attempts to eliminate Black English in schools results in a situation which can be psychologically damaging to black children.
2-	9.9305	Continued usage of nonstandard dialects of English would accomplish nothing worthwhile for society.
	9.0287	Allowing Black English to be spoken in schools will undermine the schools' reputation.
	12.8343	The scholastic level of a school will fall if teachers allow Black English to be spoken.
	6.0698	The elimination of nonstandard dialects of English is necessary for social stability.

TABLE 2. Continued.

Content and Pro/Con Black English categories	t-values	Statements
3+	10.6665	In a predominantly black school, Black English as well as Standard English should be taught.
	13.5259	Nonstandard English should be accepted socially.
	10.5426	Teachers should allow black students to use Black English in the class-room.
	8.9206	Teachers should avoid criticism of nonstandard dialects of English.
3-	10.5593	The sooner we eliminate Black English, the better.
	11.0097	The sooner we eliminate nonstandard dialects of English, the better.
	10.4839	The possible benefits to be gained from approval of Black English do not alter the fact that such approval would be basically wrong.
	13.9351	A teacher should correct a student's use of Nonstandard English.
4-	7.9740	Children who speak only Black English lack certain basic concepts such as plurality and negation.

TABLE 3. Randomized presentation order for LAS, Form 1.

Content and Pro/Con Black English categories	Number	Statements
2-	1	The scholastic level of a school will fall if teachers allow Black English to be spoken.
1-	2	Black English is a misuse of Standard English.
2+	3	Attempts to eliminate Black English in school result in a situation which can be psychologically damaging to black children.
2-	4	Continued usage of a nonstandard dialect of English would accomplish nothing worthwhile for society.
1-	5	Black English sounds as good as Standard English.
3+	6	Teachers should allow black students to use Black English in the classroom.
3-	7	Black English should be discouraged.
2+	8	Black English must be accepted if pride is to develop among black people.
1-	9	Black English is an inferior language system.
1+	10	Black English is cool.
2-	11	Black English should be considered a bad influence on American culture and civilization.
1-	12	Black English sounds sloppy.
2+	13	If use of Black English were encouraged, speakers of Black English would be more motivated to achieve academically.
1+	14	Black English is a clear, thoughtful, and expressive language.
1-	15	Black English has a faulty grammar system.
2+	16	When teachers reject the native language of a student, they do him great harm.

TABLE 3. Continued.

Content and Pro/Con Black English categories	Number	Statements
3–	17	A teacher should correct a student's use of Nonstandard English.
3+	18	In a predominantly black school, Black English as well as Standard English should be taught.
3+	19	Widespread acceptance of Black English is imperative.
3–	20	The sooner we eliminate nonstandard dialects of English, the better.
2–	21	Acceptance of nonstandard dialects of English by teachers will lead to a lowering of standards in schools.
3+	22	Nonstandard English should be accepted socially.
1+	23	Nonstandard English is as effective for communication as is Standard English.
3–	24	One of the goals of the American school system should be the standardization of the English language.
4–	25	One successful method for improving the learning capacity of speakers of Black English would be to replace their dialect with Standard English.

Data analysis. Teachers' responses were analyzed as a function of the following variables:

(1) geographical location of teaching assignment
(2) sex
(3) race
(4) field(s) of college degree(s)
(5) number of years of teaching experience
(6) grade assignment
(7) racial composition of school
(8) parents' education

Teachers' responses were submitted to a cross-tabulation computer program which allowed the viewing of each variable as a function of any other variable or group of variables. Means were then computed for each content category and the above variables to reveal the relative frequency-of-occurrence of responses in each of the five response categories.

The distribution of means across the five response categories was analyzed for each content category as a function of the sub-variables of the above variables by means of the Kolmogorov-Smirnov Test one sample. Following this operation, the Kolmogorov-Smirnov Test (two sample) was used to compare the distribution of scores across response categories for selected sub-variables of variables.

Results

Results obtained from the nationwide teacher survey are presented in Tables 4 and 5. The data are summarized as a function of each Content Category. The summaries for each category include statements on (1) the overall response pattern, (2) statistically significant main effects, and (3) statistically significant differences between selected sub-variables of main effects.

Content Category 1: Structure of Nonstandard and Black English. As shown in Table 4, there was a relatively equal distribution of teachers in the five response categories. In general, the pattern showed that 40% of the teachers responded in the two positive response categories; 40% responded in the negative response categories; and 20% revealed a neutral attitude.

Table 4 also shows that teachers in the South Atlantic rural area had significantly more negative than positive attitudes to statements in Category 1. Pacific Urban teachers, on the other hand, had significantly more positive than negative attitudes to statements in this category. None of the other geographical sub-variables was significant.

In terms of the race of teachers, black teachers revealed significantly more positive than negative attitudes toward statements in Category 1. Similarly, teachers from schools which were predominantly black had significantly more positive than negative responses. However, teachers from predominantly white schools indicated significantly more negative than positive attitudes.

Responses as a function of field of degree, years of teaching, grade taught, sex of teacher, and parents' education showed essentially flat curves with very similar proportions of Ss responding in each of the five response categories. Thus, none of the sub-variables in these areas produced significant differences in response patterns.

TABLE 4. Mean percentage of teachers responding to statements in four
Content Categories as a function of biographical variables and
response categories; and results of Kolmogorov-Smirnov one-
sample test.

Key: N = Number of observations per variable.
   * = Distribution of scores significantly different from chance.

Response categories:
   Con BE = Con Black English
   M Con BE = Mildly Con Black English
   M Pro BE = Mildly Pro Black English
   Pro BE = Pro Black English

Geography:
   SA-U = South Atlantic--Urban
   MA-U = Middle Atlantic--Urban
   ENC-U = East North Central--Urban
   ESC-U = East South Central--Urban
   WNC-R = West North Central--Rural
   SA-R = South Atlantic--Rural
   ENC-R = East North Central--Rural
   P-U = Pacific--Urban
   NE-R = North East--Rural

Content Category 1: Structure and inherent usefulness of Nonstandard
                     English Dialects

Variables	N	Con BE	M Con BE	Neither	M Pro BE	Pro BE	D	p
Overall		20.7	18.3	20.5	17.9	22.3	.02	NS
Geography								
SA-U	46	18.5	18.6	22.0	17.2	23.7	.037	NS
MA-U	36	13.4	23.7	21.8	18.0	23.2	.066	NS
ENC-U	84	24.9	20.6	22.3	18.4	13.9	.078	NS
ESC-U	30	24.8	17.9	20.0	16.9	20.5	.048	NS
WNC-R	21	9.2	26.8	28.0	20.8	13.4	.049	NS
*SA-R	37	53.7	11.6	16.5	11.5	6.7	.108	.05
ENC-R	13	34.9	29.0	10.7	15.6	9.8	.337	NS
*P-U	150	12.9	15.4	19.8	19.7	32.3	.149	.05
NE-R	6	4.2	14.6	18.8	22.9	39.6	.122	NS
Sex								
Male	80	20.3	24.6	17.4	18.0	19.7	.224	NS
Female	342	20.9	16.8	21.3	18.0	23.0	.049	NS

TABLE 4. Continued.

Variables	N	Con BE	M Con BE	Neither	M Pro BE	Pro BE	Kolmogorov-Smirnov one-sample test D	p
Race								
*Black	111	18.0	14.9	21.7	16.5	28.9	.129	.05
White	281	21.1	20.5	20.2	18.5	19.7	.018	NS
Oriental	17	23.0	10.3	20.0	18.6	28.1	.081	NS
Field								
Education	238	20.1	18.9	21.8	17.6	21.0	.024	NS
Arts-Science	35	19.0	18.5	24.6	15.5	22.4	.025	NS
Law	2	6.3	37.5	12.5	12.5	30.7	.137	NS
Business	9	33.4	19.4	8.7	16.8	18.2	.134	NS
Years teaching								
Under 1	32	14.2	15.8	22.5	20.6	26.9	.109	NS
1-2	51	14.6	18.6	18.8	18.5	29.6	.095	NS
3-5	68	15.3	14.5	23.2	18.8	28.2	.102	NS
6-10	76	25.0	19.4	18.9	16.3	20.4	.050	NS
10 years	176	25.3	19.9	20.5	17.2	17.2	.053	NS
Grade taught								
1st	178	11.3	20.5	19.4	17.7	28.6	.111	NS
2nd	40	23.0	15.2	20.6	18.3	23.0	.030	NS
3rd	38	18.9	22.3	23.1	18.5	17.2	.043	NS
4th	33	24.7	11.5	22.2	16.9	25.4	.047	NS
5th	39	15.8	22.6	18.8	20.7	22.2	.042	NS
6th	34	20.9	19.8	19.8	19.1	20.8	.009	NS
7th	5	10.0	21.9	23.8	26.3	18.1	.010	NS
8th	8	43.8	9.4	21.9	6.3	18.8	.238	NS
9th	6	59.2	19.6	15.0	0	6.3	.039	NS
10th	15	27.7	19.1	15.5	19.6	18.1	.077	NS
11th	19	37.5	20.2	16.9	16.1	9.3	.177	NS
12th	20	38.8	17.5	12.5	17.5	13.8	.188	NS
Gen. Elem.	23	13.4	19.9	26.1	19.9	20.0	.067	NS
Gen. High Sch.	1	0	0	62.5	0	37.5	.400	NS
Speech	1	0	0	12.5	25.0	62.5	.400	NS
Reading	4	9.4	27.0	38.5	9.4	15.6	.149	NS
Racial composition of school								
*Predominantly black	179	17.6	14.5	20.0	17.3	30.6	.106	.05
*Predominantly white	143	29.4	22.3	19.8	17.7	10.9	.115	.05
Mixed	48	10.8	19.9	21.3	21.4	26.7	.107	NS

TABLE 4. Continued.

Variables	N	Con BE	M Con BE	Neither	M Pro BE	Pro BE	Kolmogorov-Smirnov one-sample test D	p
Parents' education								
High school graduate	129	18.6	15.3	23.5	19.4	23.1	.61	NS
BA/BS	60	25.6	17.4	20.2	16.7	20.1	.051	NS
Graduate degree	39	13.3	16.7	24.4	15.6	30.0	.100	NS

Content Category 2: Consequences of using and accepting Nonstandard
English dialects in the educational setting

Variables	N	Con BE	M Con BE	Neither	M Pro BE	Pro BE	D	p
Overall		13.3	12.1	17.5	24.6	32.5	.172	NS
Geography								
SA-U	46	12.7	11.9	19.9	22.6	35.5	.55	NS
MA-U	36	8.7	15.4	17.9	20.6	37.3	.180	NS
ENC-U	84	15.6	16.2	17.3	28.0	21.8	.109	NS
ESC-U	30	14.8	11.9	18.2	29.3	25.8	.051	NS
*WNC-R	21	4.8	10.1	13.7	45.2	26.2	.314	.05
SA-R	37	40.1	14.4	21.9	9.9	13.7	.201	NS
ENC-R	13	14.4	23.9	19.2	25.9	16.2	.056	NS
*P-U	150	7.7	8.2	15.3	24.1	44.7	.241	.05
NE-R	6	6.3	4.2	16.7	18.8	54.2	.328	NS
Sex								
*Male	80	12.2	15.3	16.6	23.5	32.4	.159	.05
*Female	342	13.6	11.4	17.8	24.9	32.4	.172	.05
Race								
*Black	111	12.7	9.4	18.3	20.8	38.9	.204	.05
*White	281	12.6	13.7	17.4	26.3	30.0	.163	.05
Oriental	17	16.3	5.2	17.8	22.5	38.2	.207	NS
Field								
*Education	238	12.5	13.0	18.8	25.7	30.0	.157	.05
Arts-Science	35	10.4	12.2	21.9	21.5	34.1	.155	NS
Law	2	12.5	18.8	12.5	31.3	25.0	.162	NS
Business	9	32.0	19.4	11.1	13.9	23.6	.120	NS
Years teaching								
*Under 1	32	9.1	10.3	14.5	23.2	42.9	.261	.05
*1-2	51	9.1	12.3	13.8	23.5	42.4	.248	.05

TABLE 4. Continued.

Variables	N	Con BE	M Con BE	Neither	M Pro BE	Pro BE	Kolmogorov-Smirnov one-sample test D	p
Years teaching								
*3–5	68	9.7	6.9	16.9	23.4	43.1	.267	.05
6–10	76	14.6	16.3	17.1	24.7	27.3	.120	NS
*10+ years	176	17.2	13.7	18.8	26.0	24.3	.112	.05
Grade taught								
*1st	178	9.9	10.1	16.5	27.9	33.6	.235	.05
2nd	40	14.7	13.3	13.7	32.9	26.5	.183	NS
3rd	38	7.9	16.8	17.6	26.9	30.8	.153	NS
4th	33	18.2	9.9	17.1	21.0	33.8	.148	NS
5th	39	7.8	14.0	19.9	25.6	34.7	.183	NS
6th	34	7.6	14.4	20.9	21.3	35.7	.171	NS
7th	5	10.0	5.0	10.0	25.0	50.0	.350	NS
8th	8	31.3	14.1	26.6	9.4	18.8	.012	NS
9th	6	40.4	19.2	21.3	8.8	10.4	.204	NS
10th	15	20.0	10.0	16.7	27.5	25.8	.133	NS
11th	19	35.5	10.5	12.5	19.7	21.7	.155	NS
12th	20	24.8	15.2	17.0	19.0	24.0	.04	NS
Gen. Elem.	23	11.2	14.4	21.7	22.2	30.5	.144	NS
Gen. High Sch.	1	12.5	0	25.0	0	62.5	.275	NS
Speech	1	12.5	0	12.5	25.0	50.0	.035	NS
Reading	4	6.3	15.6	15.6	46.9	15.6	.181	NS
Racial composition of school								
*Predominantly black	179	11.5	8.9	14.5	23.6	41.4	.251	.05
Predominantly white	143	18.3	16.0	18.7	28.9	18.1	.070	NS
Mixed	48	5.9	21.1	15.7	21.8	40.3	.141	NS
Parents' education								
*High school graduate	129	11.6	11.8	16.7	25.9	34.0	.191	.05
BA/BS	60	16.9	9.8	20.1	19.0	34.2	.142	NS
*Graduate degree	39	9.9	7.1	16.7	28.2	40.4	.236	.05

TABLE 4. Continued.

Variables	N	Con BE	M Con BE	Neither	M Pro BE	Pro BE	Kolmogorov-Smirnov one-sample test D	p
Content Category 3: Philosophies concerning use and acceptance of Nonstandard English dialects in educational and other social settings								
Overall		16.7	17.6	17.9	20.5	24.8	.078	NS
Geography								
SA-U	46	18.9	14.3	20.6	19.3	27.0	.063	NS
MA-U	36	13.3	20.8	16.3	26.5	23.1	.096	NS
ENC-U	84	13.1	22.8	20.5	27.5	14.1	.041	NS
ESC-U	30	22.9	20.3	18.4	20.9	17.4	.032	NS
*WNC-R	21	4.8	26.2	16.7	35.7	17.9	.123	.05
SA-R	37	50.7	16.0	13.8	10.8	18.7	.307	NS
ENC-R	13	15.4	31.7	19.2	26.0	7.7	.123	NS
*P-U	150	10.3	13.2	17.3	23.2	37.1	.198	.05
NE-R	6	6.3	2.1	10.4	20.8	60.4	.412	NS
Sex								
Male	80	13.3	18.6	17.2	24.5	24.1	.109	NS
*Female	342	17.0	17.4	18.1	22.5	24.9	.075	.05
Race								
Black	111	18.5	15.3	20.8	18.9	26.6	.054	NS
*White	281	15.0	19.1	17.4	24.5	23.9	.085	.05
Oriental	17	16.7	12.1	13.8	22.8	34.6	.174	NS
Field								
Education	238	15.5	18.5	20.0	24.4	21.6	.060	NS
Arts-Science	35	14.1	17.5	21.1	18.5	28.9	.088	NS
Law	2	6.3	31.3	6.3	43.8	12.5	.161	NS
Business	9	34.7	15.3	11.1	23.6	15.3	.141	NS
Years teaching								
Under 1	32	14.5	16.5	17.0	21.0	31.0	.121	NS
1-2	51	12.4	20.4	15.1	23.6	28.5	.121	NS
3-5	68	11.5	14.3	19.7	21.0	33.9	.155	NS
6-10	76	19.8	19.4	15.5	25.8	19.5	.053	NS
10+ years	176	20.4	18.2	18.7	23.2	19.6	.027	NS
Grade taught								
1st	178	12.8	17.8	18.0	24.4	27.1	.114	NS
2nd	40	17.0	20.2	11.5	25.4	26.0	.113	NS

TABLE 4. Continued.

Variables	N	Con BE	M Con BE	Neither	M Pro BE	Pro BE	Kolmogorov-Smirnov one-sample test D	p
Grade taught								
3rd	38	10.2	20.4	21.3	30.9	17.2	.098	NS
4th	33	21.6	14.6	17.7	17.0	29.1	.091	NS
5th	39	8.8	19.9	19.1	27.8	24.4	.112	NS
6th	34	15.1	18.7	18.1	23.1	25.0	.062	NS
7th	5	20.0	20.0	17.5	17.5	25.0	.050	NS
8th	8	47.1	4.9	14.3	17.7	15.9	.271	NS
9th	6	43.3	24.6	15.4	7.0	9.6	.233	NS
10th	15	27.8	15.4	13.5	27.1	16.2	.078	NS
11th	19	35.2	19.9	12.7	17.4	14.8	.151	NS
12th	20	31.5	25.7	6.3	20.8	15.7	.172	NS
Gen. Elem.	23	10.4	18.0	23.6	23.5	24.5	.116	NS
Gen. High Sch.	1	0	0	87.5	12.5	0	.400	NS
Speech	1	12.5	0	12.5	37.5	37.5	.350	NS
Reading	4	0	24.0	26.0	25.0	25.0	.200	NS
Racial composition of school								
*Predominantly black	179	14.4	14.6	17.2	21.7	32.1	.110	.05
Predominantly white	143	20.1	23.5	18.3	25.7	12.3	.076	NS
Mixed	48	11.7	14.2	16.1	23.4	34.6	.180	NS
Parents' education								
High School graduate	129	14.2	15.6	19.0	24.3	27.1	.112	NS
BA/BS	60	21.6	14.5	18.6	19.0	26.3	.053	NS
Graduate degree	39	9.5	16.1	15.5	23.5	35.4	.199	NS
Content Category 4: Cognitive and intellectual abilities of speakers of Black English								
Overall		13.0	17.3	17.8	21.8	30.2	.121	NS
Geography								
SA-U	46	6.7	22.2	20.0	15.6	35.6	.157	NS
MA-U	36	5.6	36.1	16.7	11.1	30.6	.145	NS

190 / ORLANDO L. TAYLOR

TABLE 4. Continued.

Variables	N	Con BE	M Con BE	Neither	M Pro BE	Pro BE	D	p
Geography								
ENC-U	84	12.4	22.2	24.7	23.5	17.9	.076	NS
ESC-U	30	26.7	20.0	13.3	26.7	13.3	.062	NS
*WNC-R	21	0	19.0	0	42.9	38.1	.409	.05
*SA-R	37	41.7	25.0	13.9	11.1	8.3	.266	.05
ENC-R	13	15.4	7.7	15.4	61.5	0	.216	NS
*P-U	150	9.4	7.4	18.8	20.3	43.6	.244	.05
*NE-R	6	0	0	0	16.7	83.3	.600	.05
Sex								
*Male	80	12.7	19.0	7.6	27.8	32.9	.213	.05
*Female	342	13.0	16.9	20.1	20.4	29.6	.102	.05
Race								
*Black	111	9.2	15.6	25.7	14.7	34.9	.154	.05
*White	281	13.3	17.3	15.1	25.2	29.1	.144	.05
Oriental	17	17.6	11.8	11.8	23.5	35.3	.165	NS
Field								
*Education	238	13.2	18.0	20.5	20.9	27.4	.089	.05
Arts-Science	35	14.3	20.0	20.0	17.2	28.6	.058	NS
Law	2	0	50.0	0	0	50.0	.300	NS
Business	9	22.2	33.3	22.2	11.1	11.1	.177	NS
Years teaching								
Under 1	32	9.4	12.5	15.6	21.9	40.6	.226	NS
*1-2	51	3.9	19.6	13.7	23.5	39.2	.240	.05
*3-5	68	7.5	13.4	17.9	26.9	34.3	.213	.05
6-10	76	11.9	21.1	19.7	22.4	25.0	.081	NS
10+ years	176	20.2	18.5	17.4	19.7	24.3	.044	NS
Grade taught								
*1st	178	9.1	19.5	11.9	20.8	37.8	.197	.05
2nd	40	17.5	15.0	12.5	27.5	27.5	.150	NS
3rd	38	10.8	10.8	21.6	27.0	29.7	.184	NS
4th	33	12.1	9.1	36.4	18.2	24.2	.189	NS
*5th	39	5.1	18.0	15.4	20.5	41.0	.220	.05
6th	34	12.1	12.1	18.2	27.3	30.3	.180	NS
7th	5	0	20.0	20.0	0	60.0	.400	NS
8th	8	50.0	0	25.0	12.5	12.5	.150	NS
9th	6	40.0	40.0	20.0	0	0	.400	NS

Response categories / Kolmogorov-Smirnov one-sample test (D, p)

TABLE 4. Continued.

Variables	N	Con BE	M Con BE	Neither	M Pro BE	Pro BE	D	p
							Kolmogorov-Smirnov one-sample test	
Grade taught								
10th	15	20.0	26.7	6.7	26.7	20.0	.064	NS
11th	19	47.4	10.5	5.3	21.1	15.8	.274	NS
12th	20	20.0	30.0	10.0	25.0	15.0	.100	NS
Gen. Elem.	23	4.6	27.3	22.7	13.6	31.8	.120	NS
Gen. High Sch.	1	0	0	0	0	100.0	.800	NS
Speech	1	0	100.0	0	0	0	.600	NS
Reading	4	0	25.0	25.0	50.0	0	.200	NS
Racial composition of school								
*Predominantly black	179	13.0	10.7	15.8	17.1	42.4	.126	.05
Predominantly white	143	16.8	23.8	16.1	28.7	14.7	.050	NS
*Mixed	48	4.4	15.2	19.6	21.7	39.1	.204	.05
Parents' education								
*High school graduate	129	13.4	14.2	17.3	22.8	32.3	.160	.05
BA/BS	60	15.5	13.8	20.7	22.4	27.6	.107	NS
Graduate degree	39	5.1	23.1	10.3	23.1	38.5	.217	NS

TABLE 5. Comparisons (Kolmogorov-Smirnov Test) of results between sub-variables for national teacher LAS.

Variables compared	Statement category: 1		2		3		4	
	D	p	D	p	D	p	D	p
Sex								
M-F	.072	NS	.025	NS	.034	NS	.112	NS
Race								
B-W	.087	NS	.088	NS	.035	NS	.059	NS
W-Or.	.084	NS	.082	NS	.092	NS	.072	NS
B-Or.	.050	NS	.036	NS	.12	NS	.092	NS
Field								
Ed-A&S	.015	NS	.04	NS	.072	NS	.031	NS
Ed-Bus	.138	NS	.259	NS	.192	NS	.251	NS
Years teaching								
Less 1--3-5	.012	NS	.028	NS	.052	NS	.063	NS
3-5--10+	.178	.05	.181	.05	.14	NS	.179	.05
Less 1--10+	.163	NS	.176	NS	.118	NS	.164	NS
Race of school								
B-W	.198	.05	.181	.05	.197	.05	.147	NS
W-Mix	.210	.05	.124	NS	.222	.05	.208	NS
B-Mix	.068	NS	.078	NS	.031	NS	.086	NS
Parents' education								
HS-BA	.91	NS	.067	NS	.074	NS	.064	NS
BA-MA	.130	NS	.131	NS	.136	NS	.117	NS
HS-MA	.068	NS	.064	NS	.075	NS	.083	NS
Grade								
1-3	.136	NS	.102	NS	.082	NS	.088	NS
1-5	.090	NS	.052	NS	.040	NS	.055	NS
1-8	.290	NS	.260	NS	.245	NS	.383	.05
3-5	.071	NS	.029	NS	.072	NS	.122	NS
3-8	.403	NS	.297	NS	.369	NS	.584	.05
3-11	.186	NS	.276	NS	.250	NS	.366	NS
5-8	.280	NS	.303	NS	.383	NS	.620	.05
5-11	.217	NS	.277	NS	.264	NS	.453	.05
8-11	.093	NS	.135	NS	.119	NS	.300	NS

TABLE 5. Continued.

Variables compared	Statement category: 1		2		3		4	
	D	p	D	p	D	p	D	p
Geography								
SA[U]–MA[U]	.025	NS	.045	NS	.056	NS	.128	NS
SA[U]–ENC[U]	.083	NS	.100	NS	.109	NS	.183	NS
SA[U]–ESC[U]	.041	NS	.071	NS	.100	NS	.224	NS
MA[U]–ENC[U]	.089	NS	.145	NS	.060	NS	.124	NS
MA[U]–ESC[U]	.063	NS	.061	NS	.112	NS	.111	NS
ENC[U]–ESC[U]	.046	NS	.051	NS	.098	NS	.163	NS
SA[U]–P[U]	.116	NS	.118	NS	.129	NS	.132	NS
MA[U]–P[U]	.110	NS	.108	NS	.129	NS	.248	.05
MA[U]–NE[R]	.213	NS	.211	NS	.349	NS	.59	.05
ENC[U]–ENC[R]	.184	NS	.208	NS	.122	NS	.208	NS

Key:
  M = Male
  F = Female
  B = Black
  W = White
  Or = Oriental
  Ed = Education
  A&S = Arts & Science
  Bus = Business
  [U] = Urban
  [R] = Rural

In comparing selected sub-variables on Content Category 1, it is interesting to note that even though black teachers indicated more positive attitudes than white teachers, there was no statistically significant difference between the two groups. Similarly, there were no statistically significant differences between teachers who were of different sexes, who taught different grades, or who were from different geographical areas (even though the Pacific area produced the most favorable attitudes).

It should be noted, however, that the relatively younger teachers with three to five years experience had significantly more positive attitudes than older teachers with more than ten years experience. However, very inexperienced teachers with less than one year of experience fell in between both groups and had more neutral responses. Teachers in schools which were predominantly black had significantly more positive attitudes than teachers in schools with predominantly white student populations. Similarly, teachers in schools which had mixed student populations had significantly more positive attitudes than teachers from predominantly white schools.

Content Category 2: Consequences of using and accepting Nonstandard English. Table 4 shows that the response pattern across the five response categories for Content Category 2 reveals that teachers have more positive than negative attitudes in this area. In general, 57% of the teachers responded in the two positive categories; 25% responded in the negative categories; and 17% revealed neutral feelings.

In terms of geography, Table 4 shows that teachers in the West North Central Rural and the Pacific Urban areas had significantly more positive than negative responses in Category 2. Also, both male and female teachers indicated significantly more positive than negative attitudes in this category, as did both black and white teachers. The results for the 'field of degree' variable indicated that teachers with Education School backgrounds were the only ones to produce a statistically significant trend toward positive attitudes. It should be noted, however, that teachers with Arts and Sciences backgrounds had approximately the same distribution of attitudes as Education teachers, but significance was not realized because of the relatively small N.

In the variable category 'years teaching', all groups except the 6-10 years experience group showed significantly more positive than negative attitudes. Of all the grades sampled, only first grade teachers produced significantly more positive than negative responses. (The very large N for the first grade category probably contributed to the finding.) Similarly, only those teachers from predominantly black schools were significantly more positive than negative in their

attitudes, although teachers in schools with other racial characteristics produced non-significant trends in the same direction. Finally,
teachers whose parents were high school or graduate degree holders
had significantly more positive than negative attitudes on Content
Category 2 statements. Teachers with parents with B. A. degrees
showed a similar trend, but the N was too small to reach significance.

Comparisons of selected sub-variables reveal an interesting
difference between teachers with 3-5 years experience and those with
10 or more years experience. Teachers in the former group produced
significantly more positive attitudes than those in the latter group,
whose attitudes were approximately evenly distributed across the
five response categories. Also, a comparison of attitudes of teachers from predominantly black and predominantly white schools produced a statistically significant difference, with teachers from black
schools revealing significantly more positive attitudes than those from
predominantly white schools, who show a more even distribution of
attitudes. None of the remaining comparisons of sub-variables was
significant.

Content Category 3: Philosophies concerning use and acceptance
of Nonstandard English. Table 4 reveals that teachers' attitudes were
slightly more positive than they were negative. The magnitude of this
trend, however, was not as great as Category 2. In general, 45% of
the teachers responded in the two positive categories; 33% in the two
negative categories; and 18% were neutral.

On the geographical variable, Table 4 shows that teachers in the
West North Central Rural and the Pacific Urban areas showed significantly more positive than negative responses. Teachers in none of
the remaining geographical areas produced a significant trend. Also,
female teachers indicated significantly more positive attitudes than
males. Males demonstrated a similar pattern, but their N was too
small for significance to be reached. In terms of race, black, white,
and Oriental teachers all displayed a trend of producing more positive than negative responses to the statements in this category. However, only the result for white teachers was significant because of
their relatively large N.

Teachers in predominantly black schools also produced a significant trend toward positive responses. Teachers in predominantly
white schools demonstrated a more negative trend, though it was not
as significant. There were no significant effects obtained whatsoever
on the variables of: field of study, years teaching, or grade taught.

In comparing selected sub-variables (Table 5), significance was
achieved only for comparisons within the variable of racial composition of schools. Teachers from predominantly black schools

professed significantly more positive attitudes toward statements
from Category 3 than teachers from predominantly white schools.
Similarly, teachers from mixed schools professed significantly more
positive attitudes than teachers from predominantly white schools.
None of the remaining comparisons was significant.

Category 4: Cognitive and intellectual abilities of speakers of
Black English. Teachers demonstrated a slight trend toward positive
attitudes to the one statement from Category 4 (Table 4). Fifty-two
percent of their responses fell in the two positive response categories;
31% fell in the two negative categories; and 18% were neutral. Within
the geographical variable, Table 4 shows that teachers in the West
North Central Rural, Pacific Urban, and New England Rural areas
all produced significantly more positive than negative attitudes. However, South Atlantic Rural teachers demonstrated significantly more
negative than positive attitudes in this category.

Both black and white teachers, as well as male and female teachers, indicated significantly more positive than negative attitudes to
the statement in this response category. Also, teachers with Education School backgrounds produced significantly more positive than
negative responses. Teachers with backgrounds in other university
divisions produced a similar trend, but significance was not achieved
because of relatively small cell sizes.

On the experience variable, Table 4 shows that those with one to
two years and three to five years of experience produced significantly more positive than negative attitudes in this Content Category.
Teachers with under one year of experience and over ten years of
experience showed no significant trends away from a normal distribution.

Further, teachers in grades one and five both showed significantly
more positive than negative attitudes toward the statement in Category
4. No further significant trends were obtained in this variable. Also,
teachers from predominantly black and mixed schools both showed
significantly more positive than negative attitudes to the statement,
while teachers from predominantly white schools showed a non-
significant trend toward more negative attitudes. Finally, teachers
whose parents held high school degrees showed significantly more
positive attitudes. Teachers with parents from other education categories produced a similar trend, but the N was too small to achieve
significance. Comparisons between selected sub-variables (see
Table 4) show that teachers with three to five years of teaching experience showed significantly more positive attitudes to the statement
in this category than teachers with ten or more years of experience.
Similarly, teachers in the Pacific Urban area showed significantly
more positive attitudes than those from the Middle Atlantic Urban

area, even though teachers in the latter area had a slightly positive trend. Finally, several interesting results were achieved from comparisons of teachers at different grades. First, third, and fifth grade teachers produced significantly more positive responses than eighth grade teachers. (It should be noted, however, that grade eight had a small N.) Also, fifth grade teachers produced significantly more positive attitudes than eleventh grade teachers. None of the remaining sub-variable comparisons achieved significance.

Discussion

The most obvious finding of this survey is that teachers' attitudes relating to various topics of Nonstandard and Black English vary from topic to topic. Thus, teachers do not appear to have a single, generic attitude toward dialects, but, rather, differing attitudes depending upon the particular aspect of dialect being discussed.

Similarly, there appears to be great attitudinal variation within topic categories of Nonstandard and Black English as a function of several biographical variables. For this reason, results of such surveys should be discussed in terms of these variables, as well as the topics, if a valid picture is to be drawn.

If one were forced to make a statement about an overall trend, the best that could be said is that excluding topics dealing with the structure of Nonstandard and Black dialects, the majority of teachers throughout the country tend to reveal positive to neutral opinions. In the category pertaining to attitudes about structure, they are about evenly distributed. This finding is extremely interesting in that, contrary to popular opinion, a substantial number of American teachers are favorably disposed toward language variation, at least as measured by the present instrument. If this picture is correct, then it is obvious that school officials and language specialists have a lot of positive potential to capitalize upon to change school practices vis-a-vis dialects. In other words, enough positive attitudes seem to already be present, even though specific educational procedures and materials may be unavailable. Obviously, of course, there is a substantial core of negative attitudes which must be dealt with.

Across all four Content Categories, there were some trends related to biographical variables that are rather persuasive. Among the most important of these is the finding that teachers with three to five years of teaching experience had significantly more positive attitudes toward dialect than teachers just beginning their careers or those with ten or more years of experience. The implication of this result is that teachers who are relatively new to the teaching profession are less entrenched in their attitudes than teachers who have been teaching for long periods of time. If this finding is valid, it means that teachers with three to five years of experience are a good population for trying out new classroom procedures and methodologies. One might gather that in addition to the non-entrenchment factor, teachers in the three to five years experience category responded as they did not only because they are younger, but because they have probably been more exposed to recent thinking about language and cultural variety. If this assumption is true, then the very youngest teachers should have shown a much stronger positive trend than they did. Perhaps their relatively conservative trend was unrelated to their age or absence of new information, but, instead more related to uncertainty associated with entering the teaching profession and insecurity in trying radically different approaches.

Another overall trend is that teachers from predominantly black schools are more positive in their attitudes than teachers from predominantly white schools. It should be noted, however, that if the school population is predominantly black there is a strong chance that there are more black teachers, which may account for the trend. (It should be recalled that slightly fewer black teachers responded negatively than white teachers in all Content Categories, although significance was not achieved.) If true, however, the black teachers' non-negativeness was certainly not great enough to account for the observed trends. Also, teachers from mixed schools (which generally had white teachers) tended to be more positive than teachers in schools with a predominantly white population. The implications of the findings are clear. Teachers in schools where there were only white children, as opposed to schools where there were representative amounts of children of other races, tend to have the most negative attitudes concerning nonstandard dialects. Of course, one does not know whether these teachers went to mixed schools because they had 'liberal' attitudes on the topics or whether their attitudes developed as a result of working with children who speak nonstandard dialects on a daily basis. Both possibilities seem feasible, though other research done by this author suggests the latter as being more likely.

Implications of the present findings to the topic of bussing to achieve racial balance in schools are interesting, but frightening. The data suggest that the bussing of black children into predominantly white schools is likely to cause them to come into direct contact with teachers who are most likely to have negative attitudes toward their dialect and its use in the schools. However, given experiences with these new children, their attitudes might change to conform with those which seem to prevail for teachers in mixed schools. If true, the bussing may be more useful for the educational enrichment of the teacher than for the pupils. In any case, the whole topic needs to be reevaluated in the context of apparent attitudes on the subject.

It is interesting to note that there are no differences in attitudes between the male and female teachers on any of the response categories. Similarly, teachers did not differ significantly as a function of race, although always more black teachers were slightly more positive. This latter point is especially interesting in that it does not support numerous loosely made claims that middle class black teachers are more likely to engage in self-hate to the point that they reject their children more than white teachers. On the other hand, it is significant to note that black teachers are not as supportive of black children as some might expect, or as younger black students are, who are overwhelmingly pro-Black English. Perhaps this trend is related to age and the changing attitudes of blacks toward themselves, especially among the young. At this point, however, black teachers appear to be teachers first!

Results for geographical area comparisons are somewhat surprising on two counts. There appear to be at least two hypotheses which could be advanced to predict geographical differences in dialect attitudes. One argument would be that Southern teachers would be more positive toward black dialect than Northern teachers because there is relatively less divergence between black-white speech in the South than in the North. The other argument would posit that Northern teachers would be more positive than Southern teachers to black dialects because of different racial views, i.e. Southern teachers might be presumed to have more negative attitudes toward blacks and, therefore, more negative attitudes toward black speech. Neither of the opposing hypotheses was born out by the data.[5] Indeed there appears to be little difference between professed attitudes of Northern and Southern teachers on the topic, a fact which should lead us to talk less about regional attitudes than of national teacher trends. The only exception to this generalization would be in the Pacific Urban group which seem quite different from the other teachers, probably because they were selected from a highly cosmopolitan, 'liberal', and third-world setting in the Bay area of Northern California.

As stated, the Content Categories appear to be independent. However, attitudinal differences reflected in the categories are of importance. It has been noted, for instance, that the most negative attitudes were expressed toward the category dealing with the structure of nonstandard and black dialects while the most positive attitudes were expressed in the area of the consequences of using dialects in the schools. Thus, it appears that linguistic structure is the topic that teachers find most objectionable about nonstandard dialects. Language structure, after all, is what teachers are formally taught in schools and college, whereas positions in the other three categories are more judgmental, subjective, and less substantiated by data. In a sense, this finding is hopeful, in that the part of dialect that is most objectionable is the part that is taught to teachers, and hence, the most likely to be affected through education.

Although teachers' attitudes on structure are not positive, they are willing to profess positive attitudes toward use of different dialects in school settings. It would appear that the teachers may not like a Nonstandard dialect, but are willing to attempt to use it in hopes of finding a useful teaching tool. However, teachers' actual philosophies (or attitudes on various philosophies) are not as positive as their attitudes on consequences. For example, teachers are more likely to agree more strongly with items such as, 'When teachers reject the native language of a student, they do him great harm' than they do with items like 'Teachers should allow black students to use Black English in the classroom'. Nevertheless, most teachers are apparently open and willing to try new approaches to teaching.

There was only one item in the category concerning cognitive abilities of speakers of nonstandard dialects, thus it must be discussed with great caution. However tentative, there are some fascinating implications of the results of this survey for current tests and measures used to evaluate students' intelligence. In general, teachers seem willing to indirectly question the validity of using language foreign to the students for evaluating his IQ. In other words, given that teachers seem to recognize that language is not a valid indication of intelligence, they have implicitly called into question the validity of standardized tests which utilize Standard English as indicators of the intelligence of nonstandard speakers. Of course, most teachers do not recognize the contradiction implied by their separate views on language as unrelated to intelligence on the one hand and the primacy of Standard English on the other. Effective training should make this point clear.

NOTES

[1] The research reported in this paper was conducted as a part of a larger project conducted at the Center for Applied Linguistics and sponsored by the Ford Foundation. The author acknowledges the contributions of David Swinney, presently at the University of Texas, and Alfred Hayes, presently at Federal City College (D. C.), for their contributions to the research reported herein.

[2] Since the time of the original development of this scale, several sociolinguists have proposed more sophisticated types of approaches for assessing language attitudes, e.g. commitment type scales.

[3] A randomized presentation order for the twenty-five items in each form, as well as administration instructions, are available from the author of this paper.

[4]A map of the U.S. Census districts may be obtained from the
U.S. Census Bureau.

[5]It should be noted that the geographical hypothesis may be incapable of being tested by the present data because a substantial core
of Southern data was collected from a city which was geographically
Southern, but socially and politically Northern. Also, the geographical data may be distorted by the fact that the racial composition of
teachers' classes was not utilized in the statistical analyses. In most
cities, black teachers usually taught black students. However, Southern white teachers usually taught white students and Northern white
teachers typically taught students of all racial backgrounds. Because
of the pattern of 'de facto' segregation in teacher assignments, there
is no way to determine, for instance, whether the Southern data were
more 'liberal' because of the preponderance of black teachers with
black students and white teachers with white students.